St. Germanus
of Auxerre

by Howard Huws

Orthodox Logos Publishing

Front cover:
St Germanus of Auxerre, from an icon written for the author by
Popadija Đorđević of Novi Sad, Serbia in 2003.

© 2012, **Orthodox Logos Publishing,** The Netherlands
www.orthodoxlogos.com

ISBN: 978-90-811555-8-8

2

Contents

Plates

*(These windows and stone carving may be the earliest
known depictions of the saint.)*

Maps

Foreword

Being interested in both Orthodox spirituality and post-Roman history, I cast about for a volume presenting all that is known to us about one of the most famous and influential figures of the 5th century, Saint Germanus, Bishop of Auxerre: and finding none, have dared distil into one booklet the works of those scholars who have cast light upon one aspect or other of St Germanus' life and works.

We know more of him than of St David, St Patrick, Arthur or any other figures of the "Age of Saints", because of the singular impression he made upon his contemporaries. He is known to have visited the Isle of Britain at least once, if not twice: and his fame spread far, permeating especially into the collective memory of my own Welsh nation, amongst others. Our forefathers delighted in talk of his deeds, reminding each other of his aid and leadership in trying times. We have inherited great respect towards him, consecrating many churches and wells to God in his name, and baptizing sons in his honour.

Much has been written about St Germanus: but in the course of time, living recollection faded and gave way to distortions and embelishments. Like Arthur, he became a prop for shaky speculations, a legendary figure upon which each successive age projected its own concerns. The purpose of this little work is simply to clean the grime from his icon, leaving any restoration to more competent hands.

With that in mind, I've researched into as many sources of information as I could find, reading the works of dependable chroniclers and historians. In this I have been most generously aided by Dr Bruce Griffiths of Bangor; Dr A. C. Lake of Swansea; Tristan Grey Hulse, of Bontnewydd; and Chris Schoen of Pen-y-groes in Gwynedd, who prepared the maps. The reproductions of stained-glass depictions of St Germanus from the Cathedral of St Etienne, Auxerre, are courtesy of Professor Patrice Wahlen and Les Amis de la cathédrale St-Étienne d'Auxerre: and the picture of the image at St-Germain-l'Auxerrois, Paris, was provided by Véronique Pilon. I also thank Mr Maxim Hodak of Orthodox Logos Publishing for his skilled work and great patience.

I now present to you the poor and unworthy fruit of my labours, hoping it may cast a little more light on the saint, his faith and his times until such time as true scholars may provide its better. Should the reader find any of it to be incorrect, it his hoped he or she shall not delay in saying so: for better any error here be corrected at once, than pass for truth and infect others.

I cannot depart without drawing attention to the words of Fr Justin Popović, who stated that in reading the lives of the saints, we read the Life of Christ. Such works are a continuation of the Acts of the Apostles, and testify that the Life of Christ on this earth did not end with His Ascension into Heaven, nor with the death of His Apostles. The saints, in the Eternal Light of God, continue to direct us towards the Heavenly Kingdom: and here is the story of such a one, especially dear to us, the Welsh: Germanus, Bishop of Auxerre and friend of the Britons.

Troparion (from the French)

Holy Bishop Germanus, our defender,
Honour and comfort of the Church in Gaul
Thou didst cast off pride and wealth
So as to follow Christ our God humbly.
Thou didst combat the heresies, and ensure
The victory of the True Faith.
Father of the people of Auxerre, refuge of the unhappy,
Pray that Christ in His mercy will strengthen us.

Howard Huws.

Penrhosgarnedd.

1. The Life of Saint Germanus of Auxerre

The death of an empire is a fearful spectacle, best observed at a safe distance. While the great beast roars and thrashes in its agonies, it remains dangerous: but at its last gasps, those who once feared it will gather around, waiting their opportunity to feast off it, and so gain strength enough to fight amongst themselves for the title of Top Predator.

So it was at the begining of the fifth century AD, when the Roman Empire in the west was plunging into violence and chaos. As resources dwindled and the old imperial ideals faded, Roman commanders fought both invaders and each other for the remains of supreme authority: and having succeeded awhile, ruled cruelly and unjustly. The common folk, trodden into serfdom and taxed beyond endurance, often responded with rebellion.

At the Empire's fringes, those nations which once dreaded its power now seized their chance to carve it up. Roman dependence on German soldiers and leaders had increased considerably: but the time had now come when whole tribes could cross the frontier without hinderance. From the east bank of the Rhine, hungry eyes coveted the rich, defenceless land of Gaul.

There in Gaul, in the city of Auxerre, was Saint Germanus born to noble Christian parents in about the year 378.[1] He was well brought up, and given the best available education: and in time, was sent to Rome to study Law. On his return he began a successful career as an attorney, marrying the high-born daughter of a wealthy family, a lady of impeccable character. His career flew so high that he was appointed duke, which was honour indeed: for few could - or wished - to accept such responsibilities at so turbulent a time.[2]

Then came the unexpected. At the unanimous call of the clerics and all the people, high and low, town and country, yes, even his own colleagues, he was appointed bishop. Why? We don't know: but he himself must have been utterly convinced that his comfortable life and worldly success were as nothing compared to the opportunity to serve God and his fellow man before the holy altars. He exchanged the worldly army for that of heaven; he put off the pomp and baubles of this earth; his wife became as a sister to him; and on the seventh of July in the year 418, by popular acclaim, be was enthroned Bishop of Auxerre.[3]

He changed his way of life completely, disciplining his body by fasting and penitence. To the end of his days, he ate neither wheaten bread, oil nor beans, nor even salt: and would drink neither wine nor vinegar. He began each meal by eating some ashes, then barley bread whose grains he himself had milled.[4] Day and night, summer and winter, he wore but a mantle and tunic, whatever the weather, until they either fell to pieces or were given by him to the needy. Next to his skin he wore a prickly horsehair shirt, and he slept on a bed of a few planks and ashes, hard as the very ground. A piece of sacking beneath him answered for a mattress, and an old military cloak for a coverlet. He did without a pillow.[5]

He rarely took off his belt or shoes, and around his neck wore a leather thong bearing a small box of relics. Such discomfort meant that he could barely sleep, but by penitence and prayer his sanctity was burnished as if by long, slow martyrdom. He remained most welcoming and hospitable, feeding all who came to him, and washing their feet. He achieved that which is most difficult: to live like a hermit in the midst of daily distractions, and as if in the desert, within sight and reach of all the world's pleasures. After a short while he founded a monastery near the city, on the opposite bank of the river, so that the Church, through this community, could spread the Orthodox Christian faith among the local inhabitants.[6]

By the Grace of God, and his untiring efforts, signs were given that Germanus was indeed a conduit of divine power. Ianuarius the regional tax-collector, visiting the bishop one Saturday, was so careless as to lose his satchel of monies. He took his eyes off it for a moment, and in that instant it was stolen by a man possessed by a demon. When Ianuarius discovered his loss, he was beside himself with fear and fury: and in his terror, demanded that Germanus repay him every last coin, as if the bishop was to blame.

"In God's name", said the bishop, "I promise you'll get the money back". But by the following Sunday there was no sign of the satchel, and the tax-collector was on his knees before Germanus, wailing that the Governor would kill him if the lost money wasn't found.

"Patience", said the bishop, "all will be well."

Before attending liturgy that morning, Germanus requested a private interview with that unfortunate man who'd stolen the money. The bishop demanded that he confess his misdeed immediately, but the demon controlling him refused point blank. His ire aroused, Germanus went to the church, where he commanded that the demoniac be brought before the congregation. There the bishop prostrated himself, and prayed.

At once, the thief was hurled up into the air, and began to scream deafeningly. As if on fire, he shouted that he'd stolen the money. After Germanus had quizzed him further, the taxman's gold was found, and the demon cast out of the poor sufferer. Germanus had healed many before that time, but in secret: this was one of the few times he did so in public.

Then the city was stricken by a disease of the throat, which first killed children, then their parents. With his flock decreasing by the day, Germanus sensed that the powers of evil were behind this plague: so he blessed oil, and anointed each sufferer in turn. The sickness abated at once: and as one of the demons fled, it yelled that they, the spirits of evil, had caused the disease, and that the prayers of the holy man had seen them off.

Another time, whilst Germanus was returning to the monastery from a journey, one of the monks there began prophesying that the bishop wouldn't be able to cross the river to them for lack of a boat. After a while, the bretheren went down to the waterside, and indeed, the "prophet" was right. So a boat was despatched to fetch the bishop home, and when he landed, they told him how they knew of his return. Germanus sensed that this prophetic ability was not God's doing, but the Devil's: for the Evil One too has spiritual power, and can send prophecies and visions in order to mislead men, and tighten his grip upon us. He immediately exorcised the "prophet" of the demon in him: and in a foul stench, the unclean spirit fled.

Whilst journeying late one winter's evening, Germanus and his party reached an old ruin which local people said was haunted. It had fallen into almost total decay: but as soon as the bishop heard mention of ghosts, he insisted on staying there. One fairly complete room was found, so they laid their packs there, and all except Germanus ate a little. At the darkest hour, with the bishop now asleep, one of the clerics began to recite according to his office: but suddenly, a fearsome spectre appeared before him, and a shower of stones pelted the walls. In terror, the reader called on Germanus, who awoke instantly. He arose, looked into the spectre's eyes, and ordered it to state, in the name of Christ, who it was, and why it haunted that place.

Cowering, the ghost told Germanus that when alive, it was one of a pair of robbers who had been killed, and their bodies dumped there like so much rubbish. Denied peaceful rest, they disturbed the living: and it begged the bishop to pray to the Lord, that He would take them to Him, and grant them eternal repose.

12

The saint knew well that human bodies, the image of the Almighty, should never be so mistreated, whoever they were. He ordered the spectre to show him where the bodies lay, and by torchlight, despite the foul weather and the dilapidation, the ghost indicated the very spot. At dawn, the bishop asked assistance of some of the neighbours, exhorting them to shift the rubble: and there were found the two corpses, still manacled. A grave was opened, the manacles removed, shrouds were wrapped about the remains, and a Christian burial conducted. In giving peace to the dead, quiet was granted to the living: for the ruin was repaired, and henceforth became a tranquil home.

Germanus proceeded on his way: and whist staying, as he preferred, at poor lodgings, he spent the night in prayer. At dawn, he noticed that the farmyard cockerels were silent: so he enquired regarding this strange behaviour. The answer given was that they hadn't crowed for many a day: could he help them? The bishop took wheat, blessed it, and fed it to the tongue-tied birds: and ever afterwards, they greeted the sunrise most enthusiastically. A small matter: but sufficient to reveal the greatness of the Lord.[7]

As the western half the Empire collapsed, the Emperor Honorius told the Britons to look to their own military defence. The islanders, however, remained in contact with their continental neighbours: and in the year 429 a deputation of them arrived in Gaul seeking aid against spiritual enemies. The followers of the heretic Pelagius were abroad in their land, and successfully spreading their misleading ideas amongst both cerics and laymen. The unity of the Christians, and their relationship with the Catholic Church, the very Body of Christ, were in dire peril.[8]

Who was Pelagius? A Briton, it's said, who preached in Rome at about the begining of the fifth century. His notion was that anyone could save his or her own soul by virtue of works alone. All that was necessary to secure salvation, he thought, was to use our free will in order to differentiate between good and evil. Easy? Too easy by half: it would mean that the definition of "good" and "evil" would depend entirely on one's own whims. Christ's coming, death and ressurection would be effectively redundant. Also, any "success" on our part would invite pride, the chief of sins: and any "failure" would throw us into hopeless despair.

The truth is that man must co-operate with God in order to be saved. Yes, we've been granted free will: but without God's Grace, we'd misuse our freedom to wander off-course into the darkness, as Adam did. Only by co-operating with God, by asking His support and that His Grace light our path and steer our will towards salvation, despite our sins, can we be saved. For if, by the light of Grace, we use our free will to move one step towards God, He'll take ten steps toward us, just as the father ran to greet the prodigal son. That's the truth which Pelagius was undermining.

The news from Britain horrified the shepherds of the Catholic Church in Gaul. A synod of bishops was convened, and it was decided to send bishops Germanus of Auxerre and Lupus of Troyes to Britiain, to preach against the Pelagians and reinforce Christian unity. So

14

they set out together for the coast.[9]

Seeing both men sailing for Britain, demons brewed so terrible a storm that both clouds and waves were churned into a howling, crashing tempest. The sailors feared that the ship would surely be sunk: but with the vessel being tossed on the sea like a cork, Germanus went to sleep. If it was bad before, it now became ten times worse: and Lupus and the others woke the saint, begging him to help them. Germanus kept both his cool and his faith: and in the Name of Christ, he reprimanded the waves. Pouring a little oil on the waters, he prayed: and the storm ceased, the sea became calm, and both bishops landed safely in Britain.

They were welcomed there by crowds of people from near and far, because unclean spirits, possessing a number of unfortunates, had prophesied the coming of the Gaulish bishops. Germanus and Lupus cast those spirits out: and in fleeing, they roared that they were the ones responsible for raising such a hurricane against the Lord's servants.

The two bishops had so much success in preaching against the Pelagians that report of them and their miracles ran from one end of the island to the other. With enormous crowds pressing upon them, they preached in churches and at crossroads, in the fields and lanes, encouraging the faithful and bringing the lost back into the fold. By spoken and written word, and by miracles, entire regions were brought back to the True Faith. The Pelagians saw their support vanishing like April snow, and when it was suggested that a public debate between both parties be held, the heretics accepted the challenge, thinking to silence the Catholic bishops once and for all.

The Pelagians and their supporters arrived at the appointed place in rich attire, hoping to create an impression.[10] They opened their mouths to lecture: but no amount of fine clothing could disguise their lack of understanding. Against them stood Germanus and Lupus, men well trained in debate, skilful and eloquent speakers, and more importantly, men illumined and convinced by the Truth. By inspired preaching, and quoting the Scriptures, they quashed their opponents and demolished their arguments in no time. The crowd could scarcely be prevented from tearing the Pelagians to pieces: but no-one could stop their deafening cheers for the two bishops.

Suddenly, a military officer stepped into the ring, placing his blind, ten year old daughter in the bishops' arms, and asking them to restore her sight. [11] "Take her to our opponents", said they. In fear, the Pelagians refused to attempt such a thing. Rather, they joined in the people's call that the bishops heal her. Germanus prayed a little: then took the box of relics from about his neck, and touched her eyes with it. Her sight was restored to her at once: and as her parents called out their thanksgiving, the crowd was awestruck, seeing that the Bishop of Auxerre's strength lay not only in words, but in his indefatigable faith. From then on the people flocked to Germanus and Lupus, not to the Pelagians.

As he was in Britain, Germanus saw fit to visit the grave of the Holy Martyr Alban.[12] On the way, however, a demon caused him to fall and hurt his foot, and he was

16

confined to bed. By accident, one of the nearby houses caught fire: and as they were thatched with dried reeds, the flames soon spread to all other buildings in the neighbourhood. Germanus' friends rushed to the rescue, but he refused to let them move him, reprimanding them for their lack of faith. So they ran to save what they could: but all was consumed. Every building, that is, except the one in which Germanus lay. Though fire surrounded it, not one reed was burnt: and when the flames were extinguished, it yet stood a whole house in a sea of ashes. Germanus was none the worse.[13]

Talk of him spread throughout the surrounding countryside, and people thronged to him in hope of healing. Despite which, he never allowed anyone to try and cure him: rather, he patiently awaited the Lord's mercy. One night, he saw a shining man in the whitest garments reach out to him, ordering him to arise and stand. He obeyed: and having arisen, found that his foot was completely healed. He could resume his journey.

Lent came: that time of year when Christians give particular attention to the quality of their spiritual life, and enter into training for Easter. Unfortunately, it was also a time when the Britons' enemies were giving particular attention to attacking them. The Picts and Saxons had been raiding for decades, bringing bloodshed and ruin wherever they struck. Now they decided to unite as an unstoppable horde, to pillage and kill on an even greater scale: and so they descended upon the land like countless wolves.

There were no Roman legions to stop them. There were

17

brave men, but no-one who could lead and inspire them in the face of this threat. They turned to Germanus, and he accepted the challenge: to forge an army, and lead it against the foe. Eager to become trained soldiers, warriors flocked to hear him preach, and to be baptised by him. In their camp they erected a church of green boughs in preparation for Easter, and with the Picts and Saxons approaching, Germanus there celebrated the Great Feast. Then, being their General, he inspected the defences, and led part of his force towards the mountains which stood between the Britons and their enemies. With practised eyes he picked out the path by which the barbarians would probably pass between the hills, and down a steep valley. He ordered his soldiers to hide themselves: no-one was to move or make the least sound until he gave the sign.

As he foresaw, so it happened. The enemy crept over the pass, thinking to fall on the Britons' camp in a surprise attack.

Suddenly, Germanus and Lupus stood before them, and shouted: "Hallelujah!"

"Hallelujah!" shouted the soldiers, leaping out of their cover on either side of the astounded foe.

"Hallelujah!" shouted the bishops again.

"Hallelujah!" yelled the Britons, waving their arms and banners.

"Hallelujah!" a third time.

18

"Hallelujah!" until the very rocks rang.

The Picts' and Saxons' hearts failed, their guts turned to porridge within them, and their blood ran cold. As one man, they turned to flee, throwing their arms and booty as they raced back for the hills, with the Britons in hot pursuit. Such was their panic, many were drowned in trying to cross a nearby river. Victory went to Germanus, with not a drop of British blood shed.[14]

Having defeated enemies spiritual and earthly, Germanus and Lupus returned home. By virtue of their goodness, and by the entreaties of the Holy Martyr Alban, they had a safe passage: but on reaching Auxerre, Germanus saw that his fellow-citizens were in difficulties indeed, ground down and impoverished by additional new taxes. Full of compassion, he decided to go to the governor and ask for the lifting of this burden from the people: and so a small deputation started out for Arles, the regional capital, with Germanus riding the worst of the nags.[15]

On the way south, an apparently impoverished traveller joined the group. No-one knew he was a thief, and that night, whilst the others prayed, he made off with the bishop's horse. The following morning, with both "traveller" and nag gone, one of the priests offered his own mount to Germanus, and they set off again. It was noticed that the bishop was doing his best not to laugh: and one of his comrades asked him what he found amusing, considering that a thief had stolen his horse.

"Let's wait awhile", said the bishop, "because truly, that poor man's in a real fix. You'll see him now, all of a lather."

At that, who ran towards them but the thief himself, leading the missing horse. He prostrated himself at Germanus' feet, confessing that he'd taken the animal and tried to ride it, but it wouldn't budge an inch. Then when he attempted to dismount, he couldn't: he was stuck fast in the saddle, and could only move when he decided to restore to the bishop his horse.

Germanus said: "Had we given to you according to your needs, you wouldn't have been driven to steal. Take now what you require, and render to us our property." Because he'd confessed, the thief obtained reward and blessings, rather than punishment.

Though he tried to travel inconspicuously, talk of his miracles went before him, and crowds came to greet him all along the way, eventually forming one long procession. He stayed awhile at Alise with his old friends, the priest Senator and Nectariola his wife.[16] Seeing Germanus' bed so uncomfortable, Nectariola (unbeknown to the bishop) discreetly placed some straw beneath it, to soften it somewhat. Having spent the night in prayer and chanting psalms, Germanus resumed his journey the following morning, and Nectariola carefully kept the straw.

A few days later, a local nobleman, Agrentius, was possessed by a demon from which no-one could release him. Nectariola remembered the straw, and arranged that Agrentius be wrapped in it. He screamed Germanus' name all that night, but by dawn the demon had left him once and for all.[17]

20

As sailing downriver was easier than following the rough roads, Germanus was borne down the Saône to the city of Lyons.[18] He was warmly welcomed there, and agreed to stay awhile, healing and preaching during that time. Then onwards to Arles, where he was received by its pious and hard-working Bishop Hilarius.[19] Auxiliaris the governor arranged to meet the visitor at once, as he wished Germanus to heal his wife, who was suffering from a fever. He offered presents and all manner of services to the Bishop of Auxerre, if only he'd free her from her infirmity. So it was: she was completely cured by him, and consequently, due to Germanus' supplications on behalf of his fellow-citizens, the governor agreed to abolish the extra taxes on the inhabitants of Auxerre. Good news, indeed: but better still, in their eyes, was their bishop's return home to them at the conclusion of his task.

In the meantime, a messenger had arrived from Britain, asking once again for help against the Pelagians. The heretics, given a breathing space, had begun to mislead innocent Christians again. The Gaulish bishops begged Germanus to go there once more: and without hesitation, he returned to Britain accompanied by Severus, Bishop of Trier.[20] This time, the voyage went well.

As before, unclean spirits had possessed some Britons, leading them to prophesy the bishops' coming to the chieftain Elafius. He and his entire province hurried to greet Germanus and Severus on the shore. Germanus could see that most people had kept the Faith, and that the remaining Pelagians were but a few. They were quickly identified and condemned.

Elafius had bought with him his son, who had suffered from childhood from a withered leg to the degree that it was quite useless. Now the chieftain begged the bishops' aid. Germanus had the boy sit. His hand touched all the stricken parts of the leg, and in front of all there, the tight sinews relaxed, strength returned to the feeble muscles, and the chieftain's son was healed. The people's faith was confirmed, and Germanus and Severus went on to preach successfully against the heretics. It was decided to exile Pelagius' followers from the island, and that the bishops should send them to the Continent so that Britain would be rid of them once and for all.[21] So successful were the two bishops that the Faith remains spotless in those parts to this day: and having completed their mission, both men returned home.[22]

But as soon as Germanus reached Auxerre, another deputation sought him out. They were from Armorica: and as punishment for a recent rebellion there, Aëtius, effective ruler of the Empire in the west, had told Goar, king of the Alans, to ravage the area and despoil its inhabitants.[23] The Armoricans begged the bishop's help, and that he defend them by force of words and faith from this disaster. One old bishop against a fearsome pagan tribe: but Germanus of Auxerre was no ordinary man.

He needed to act quickly, and hurried to the Alan camp before they could reach and destroy Armorica. It was easy enough to find, the roads being crowded with armed warriors heading in that direction. Germanus went directly to Goar, and speaking through an interpreter, humbly asked him to hear his pleas on behalf of the Armoricans. Goar wasn't interested: booty lay before him, and he ignored the bishop completely. He continued to snub him until Germanus grabbed hold of his horse's bridle and physically stopped him and his army from going a step further.

A brave act: Goar could easily have drawn his sword, and lopped off Germanus' hand there and then for daring to touch the bridle. But if the Alans didn't respect priests, they respected bravery: and Goar was so astounded that he agreed to discuss the matter with this courageous Christian. As a result, he undertook to take no action against the Armoricans if Aëtius and the Emperor should agree to forgive the rebels their disobedience.

So Germanus took the road to Italy, to the Emperor's court at Ravenna.[24] Arriving at Alise once again on his way, he miraculously healed a mute, twenty year old girl, anointing her with oil and giving her three pieces of bread soaked in wine and spices to eat: and so she spoke for the first time in her life. He called by Senator, and when leaving the city, Germanus embraced his old friend, saying: "May God permit we meet again on the Day of Judgement, for we'll not meet again in this world."

Proceeding onwards, vast crowds came to greet him, especialy at Autun where he healed a girl who had been born with her hand clenched tightly into a fist, so that her fingernails grew through its flesh.[25] He himself loosened the sinews and muscles, before trimming her nails to the usual length. Then on through the Alps, a wild and dangerous region, where the saint set an example by carrying an old, lame traveller's load over a deep mountain stream, before carrying the traveller himself

23

over on his own back.

Having reached Milan, Germanus did his best not to attract attention.[26] In vain, for on the feast of the city's saints, a man possessed by a demon shouted out: "Germanus, why do you pursue us to Italy? Isn't it enough that you drive us from Gaul? Take a rest, and leave us be!" That was enough to start people asking questions, and looking about them: and the famous Bishop of Auxerre was soon recognised, despite his shabby appearance. They asked him to cast the demon out of the man, and so he did. The unclean spirit was put to flight, and once again folk flocked to Germanus to be healed, and to hear him preach.

Following that, the travellers made for the rising sun, eastwards towards the Adriatic coast, and Ravenna. Coming across three beggars on the roadside pleading for alms, Germanus asked his deacon:

"How much is there in the purse?"

"Three gold pieces", he replied.

"Give them the three pieces", ordered the saint.

But the deacon only gave them two, lest some need befall the bishop's retinue. Proceeding, they were greeted by the servants of a man named Leoporius, who begged Germanus to attend their master, that he and his family should be healed. The bishop agreed, and though it meant going out of his way, he said: "Nothing should come before doing the Lord's will". And at that, the servants handed him a present of two hundred gold pieces.

"Take the money," said Germanus to his deacon, "and remember that you cheated the poor. Had you obeyed me, these men would have given us three hundred gold pieces, not two hundred." He followed the servants to Leoporius' house and healed all there, master and servants, rich and poor, and stayed the night under that roof.[27]

After his experiences in Milan, Germanus was determined to arrive at Ravenna discreetly. He waited until nightfall before venturing near, but in vain: the watchmen had remained awake in order to await him, and a great welcome had been prepared by Bishop Peter, the Empress Placidia, and her son Valentinian, faithful Catholics and hearers of God's priests.[28] The nobles vied for Germanus' favour, and the Empress sent him an enormous silver platter loaded with food. He kept the gift, sharing the meal among his retainers and making of the silver alms for the poor. He sent her a barley loaf in a wooden dish, of which she was so proud that she had the dish covered in gold, and the loaf reserved for healing many of the sick.[29]

As the streets were thronged with people trying to catch a glimpse of him, Germanus had to use the backstreets if he was to arrive anywhere on time. On such an occasion he passed by the city jail, and those there awaiting torture or execution cried out to him for mercy and help. The bishop sent for the prison officers, but they refused to come, as the penalties had been set the previous evening by palace officials. Germanus walked up to the jail, and in full view

25

of all, prostrated himself in prayer. At that, the prison gates swung agape of themselves, the chains fell from the manacles, and the sturdy bolts shot open. The prisoners walked free. All came to the saint, and accompanied him in procession to the church.[30]

People flocked to him every day, and six bishops were continually in his company. Volusianus (secretary to the nobleman Sigisvult) and his wife came to him, begging him to heal their son, who was suffering from a burning fever. He accompanied them to their home: but was then informed that the lad had died. All turned to Germanus, entreating him to pray for the Lord's mercy upon the youth and his parents: and he agreed to do so, though with reluctant modesty. He sent all from the room, and having stretched himself out on the corpse in prayer and with many tears, behold, in a short while the youth began to stir somewhat, and open his eyes, and then speak. And gradually, God granted him complete health.[31]

The Royal chamberlain, Acolus the eunuch, had an adopted son who was possessed by a devil. The boy was sent to Germanus for healing, but he deferred the matter until the following day, so competely in thrall to the demon was the young man's body. The bishop ordered he be kept in the same room as him overnight, so that an exorcism could be performed: and after the unclean spirit had revealed itself, and admitted that it had possessed the innocent youth since childhood, Germanus succeeded in casting it out, once and for all.

In the meantime the Armorican leader Tibatto had excited his people into further rebellion, thwarting Germanus'

26

attempt to obtain them forgiveness. The Emperor sent his forces to that land, and Tibatto was defeated and executed.[32]

One day, Germanus told his fellow-bishops that he'd dreamt that the Lord's hand had given him a gift of traveller's necessities. At which, he'd asked why these had been granted to him.

"Fear not", came the reply, "I'm not going to send you on another exhausting journey. This will be an easy trip to a land where you'll find peace and eternal rest." Though the other bishops tried to offer another interpretation, Germanus said: "I well know what country the Lord promises His servants."

A few days later, the saint fell ill, to the great consternation of all the people. To comfort him, the Empress asked him to name whatever he desired.

"The return of my remains to my own homeland", he replied.

In the midst of many people praying and chanting psalms, Germanus lay seven days ill. Then, in accordance with his dream, his faithful and blessèd soul departed for heaven.[33]

His few posessions were shared out. The Empress took the small reliquary which hung about his neck. Bishop Peter took his mantle and his hair shirt, and the other six bishops the remainder of his clothes: his episcopal mantle, his belt, the old military cloak, and his tunic. Acolus the

Chamberlain paid for anointing the body with spices, and the Empress for burial vestments suitable for a bishop. The Emperor supplied the bier and all else necessary for the journey, and a great throng of his servants to accompany Germanus. So the saint's relics were carried from town to town all five hundred and fifty miles from Ravenna to Auxerre.

At Piacenza, the relics were deposited overnight in a church.[34] A paralyzed woman asked to be placed under the bier: and when it was lifted the following morning, she could stand on her feet and follow it.[35]

In Gaul, all competed to honour the relics, and to ensure them a smooth journey by repairing roads, restoring bridges, singing psalms, lighting torches and bearing the load on their own shoulders. So Germanus' earthly remains were brought home on the twenty-second of September.[36]

He was buried at Auxerre on the first day of October, and his eternal soul now stands before God, interceeding ceaselessly for all who ask his help. Amen.

Notes

1) Auxerre, the Autessiodunum of the Romans, is a city about 93 miles south-east of Paris. Germanus' name could indicate that he was of Teutonic descent, but it was by no means uncommon. Ifor Williams doubted whether the Welsh name "Garmon" could be derived from "Germanus",

but noted that the words "*garm*" (Welsh) and "*gairm*" (Irish) mean "a shout" (see note 13 below). Henry Lewis, however, demonstrated that "Germanus" could become "Garmon" without transgressing any linguistic rules. In the subregion of Armorica, the cities of Auxerre, Sens, Paris, Chatres, Troyes, ac Orléans fell within the administrative unit of Lugudunesis Senonia.

Note that Germanus, Bishop of Paris (496-576) is quite another person. The similarity of name and location subsequently caused quite some confusion. Others of the same name include Germanus, St Jerome's companion on his visits to the Egyptian hermits, and Germanus the Daco-Roman, friend (and perhaps relative) of St John Cassian (see Chapter 4), honoured by the Orthodox in Romania.

2) It's possible that Saint Germanus had received military training and responsibilities during his earthly career. Constantius calls him *ducatus culmen*, which usually signifies a military leader: and in mentioning "more than one region", he probably has Armorica and Nervica in mind. Roughly, that is, the area between the Garonne and the east bank of the Seine, and present-day Belgium. Note also Constantius' mention of "leaving the earthly army in order to join the heavenly", and other possible hints in the text (see notes 5 and 13 below). The title *Dux*, however, could indicate a leader or guide of any kind. Blessèd Augustine (*Confessions*, Book IX) gives the

example of his friend Euodius, who left off earthly warfare and girded himself unto God's.

Constantius also states that Germanus held the civil office of *regimen per provincias*, and this creates a problem: for at that time, one could not hold both military and civil offices simultaneously. However, the account of Germanus' military exploit in Britain, and his diplomatic feats amongst the Alans, and at Arles and Ravenna, could indicate that the saint's experience was wider than usual.

3) At that time, should a man's fellow-citizens appoint him to an office, he would feel bound to accept the responsibility at once, and perform his duties to the utmost of his ability. St Ambrose, in the same manner, found himself Bishop of Milan; St Cyprian, Bishop of Carthage; Synesius, Bishop of Ptolemais, and St Martin, Bishop of Tours. The practice was so widespread as to appear conventional.

Germanus' predecessor as Bishop of Auxerre was Amator. He, and Victricius, Bishop of Rouen (who visited Britain in 396) were St Martin of Tours' most prominent disciples. Amator died in 418.

4) See the *Life of St John of Colonia*, by Cyril of Scythopolis, for another example of eating ashes. Also Psalm 102:10 (LXX).

5) Barley was considered food fit for horses, paupers and prisoners. Constantius calls Germanus' mantle a *sagulum*, which usually means a general's cloak. St Martin of Tours had similar tastes in bedding, according to Sulpicius Severus' *Letter to Eusebius*.

6) Early Christianity was a largely urban faith in the west, *pagan* meaning, literally, a "country man". The *Life of St Martin of Tours* testifies that some (if not most) natives held to the old gods, and most barbarian incomers were either pagans or Arians. This monastery was initially consecrated in the name of the holy unmercenaries Cosmas and Damian, but later took the name of Marianus, a monk who expired there.

7) Saints' lives often feature the subject in harmony with animals, sanctity entailing a return to man's prelapsarian condition: see Cogitosus' story of St Bridget and the fox in his *Life of St Bridget*, for example. This particular feat of St Germanus', however, appears to have led to his being regarded as patron saint of domestic chickens, in sixteenth-century England, at least. A passage in John Bale's *Comedy Concernynge Thre Lawes*, satirizing the Catholics' appeal to specific saints for aid against specific ills, goes as follows:

> With blessynges of Saynt Germyne,
> I will me so determyne,
> That neyther foxe nor vermyne,
> Shall do my chuckens harme.

For your duckes seynte Lenarde...

8) The date of Christianity's arrival in Britain is not
    known. Old Greek texts state that the Apostle
    Aristobulus brought the Faith hither: but in listing
    provinces where Christians were found, Justin
    Martyr (c.150 AD) doesn't name this island.
    Neither does Irenaeus of Lyons in his list of c.180
    (*Adversus Haereses I.23*). Shortly after the year 200,
    Tertulian (in Carthage) in his *Adversus Judaeos*
    mentions "places of the Britons not reached by the
    Romans, but under the rule of Christ", and that
    the "name of Christ rules there". About the same
    time, Origen (in Alexandria) mentions Britian
    when stating that Christianity had reached the
    ends of the civilized world (*Sermons IV, VI and
    XXVIII*). Hyperbole, perhaps: but both cities were
    on the busy and well-established trade routes
    which carried information from one end of the
    Empire to the other, and the writers' reputations
    depended on their adherence to what was known
    or presumed to be true, however much they
    elaborated upon it.

    Eusebius' words (*De Mart. Palest. XIII. 10,11*)
    regarding Constantius Chlorus' reluctance to
    persecute Christians may be evidence that they
    were in Britain by c.293-306 AD. The presence of
    three bishops, a priest and a deacon from Britain at
    the Synod of Arles in the year 314 suggests that
    the Church was well-established here by the
    begining of the fourth century.

Regarding Pelagius and his notions, see Chapter 4 below.

9) It would be natural for those Britons worried by the presence of Pelagians or other foes to appeal for spiritual or military help to that part of the "Catholic" Empire nearest to them, i.e. the very provinces of Armorica and Nervica of which Germanus was a leader (see Chapter 4 below). Regarding St Lupus, see Chapter 5 below.

If an episcopal synod was held before sending Germanus and Lupus to Britain, this is the only surviving reference to it. According to the *Life of St Lupus* (a later document which is judged not to be, in itself, a dependable historical source), Germanus and he sailed for Britain in winter, as suggested by the foul weather mentioned in the *Life of St Germanus*. They would have had to sail by March at the latest, in order to have accomplished all that was done in Britain before celebrating Easter here.

Polemius Silvius, writing in the year 449, states that Boulogne (Bolonia) was the chief port of embarkation for those travelling from the Continent to Britain. Constantius doesn't mention it by name, but compare its geographical location with his mention of "tender breezes from the Bay of Gaul". De Plinval refers to a tradition that St Germanus sailed from Saint-Germain-des-Vaux, 20 kilometres west of Cherbourg, perhaps in order to avoid the Franks who had newly settled on the north bank of the Seine. De Plinval's opinion is that Germanus and Lupus crossed the channel to Britain at the end of summer 429, spending seven months here before returning to Gaul immediately after Easter 430. In Britain, the chief port of embarkation for the Continent was Richborough.

10) It has been argued that the mention of sumptuous clothing suggests that Pelagianism was fashionable amongst the local aristocrats, as in Rome (despite some Pelagians' enmity towards the rich); that what Constantius describes here is an assembly of civic dignitaries in ceremonial robes; or even that some British nobles, having seized power and severed connections with the Empire, had adopted Pelagianism to further stress the political difference between them and the Catholic supporters of the Empire. However, there's no hard evidence of that: and care should be taken in perceiving connections between social trends, political opinions, and historical events on the one hand, and theological or religious disputes on the other, especially where evidence to that effect is scarce (as in 5th-century Britain).

Religion is strongest at the personal level, and uncertainty regarding the state and fate of the soul, and those of our family and acquaintances, is more likely to stimulate the believer in us than are meditations concerning the nature of contemporary politics and who holds which position of influence. By all means let us interpret the past in the light of present knowledge: but beware also of projecting our own opinions onto the past, thus causing it to reflect what we wish to see.

Having said that, it must be admitted that religion in all ages has powerful attractions not directly spiritual. To the selfish, it may be a means of gaining wealth or political power. To those bereft of confidence in the political order, as in the case of a failing state, it can provide an alternative means of defining one's identity, i.e. that people prefer to identify with a religious group or party than with that state. Those seeking a glimpse of the attitudes of 5th-century Britons may care to look at present-day Afghanistan or Nigeria, where the collapse of empire and the failure of native governments have stimulated the growth of strong religious movements at the expense of state power.

Perhaps Constantius underlines the contrast between the ascetic Germanus and his well-dressed opponents in order to ridicule the Pelagians, and the inherent pride of those who think that man has no need of Christ's sacrifice. Could Constantius also be echoing the words of Book 1 of St Jerome's *Dialogus contra Pelagi*?:

"Beware, you clerics; beware, you monks: widows and virgins, you are in peril unless the people see you dirty and dressed in rags. I say nothing of laymen, who declare open war upon God, and enmity towards Him, if they wear smart, expensive clothes."

35

Where in post-Roman Britain would such am assembly have been held? London, perhaps, where the remains of a very substantial late fourth- or early fifth-century basilica have been found? If so, were Germanus and Lupus active in the area of Kent? Archaeological evidence, including the Christian wall paintings at Lullingstone and what appears to be a sumptuous baptistery at Bax Farm, suggests that Christianity was comparatively strong in the London-Richborough district in the late Roman period. The large number of villas there also suggests wealthy communities whose leaders could well have afforded fine apparel. St Albans would be a possible location, as it's named immediately following this episode: but the text suggests a journey or intervening period between the public debate and reaching that city.

In what language did Germanus and Lupus preach? Linguistic evidence suggests that the Latin of the educated British aristocracy was unusually, even rather archaically correct, as regards pronunciation: but as Latin seems not have enjoyed much currency beyond urban and military centres, how could the "enormous crowds" who listened to the two bishops have comprehended them?

A slender suggestion is provided by Sidonius Apollinaris' Third Epistle. Writing in about the third quarter of the 5th century, he praises his brother-in-law for inducing the nobles of Gaul to abandon "the barbarous Celtic dialect". If by that sneer he means the Gaulish language, then he testifies that it was spoken by the social élite until as late as that time. It is not wholly inconceivable, therefore, that both Germanus and Lupus, decades previously, could also have spoken Gaulish.

Gaulish was a Celtic tongue, closely related to the Brittonic spoken in Britain at that time. Additionally, it is known that certain tribes from present-day northern France and Belgium had migrated to Britain shortly before the Roman conquest, settling, for the most part, in the southeast of the island. They would presumably have retained much of their own way of speech, were it different to that of other Britons. Would it be beyond reason to suggest that Germanus and Lupus, arriving from northern Gaul four hundred years later, could have made themselves understood in that same south-eastern part of the island?

Constantius' statement about preaching in rural areas is interesting. Sts Martin and Victricius did so in Gaul because Christianity was an urban faith there, and the rural areas pagan. In Britiain, the little surviving evidence has led some to suggest that the situation was different: that Christianity was at its most popular in small towns and the countryside. Others maintain that all that can be safely said is that Christianity was strongest in the south-east of the island, and in the army.

11) A "man with tribunician power", writes Constantius. The title of "tribune" was first claimed by the earliest Roman emperors, but was bestowed, by Germanus' time, on military officers in general.

12) Gildas states that the holy martyr was a native of St Albans (Verulamium) in Hertfordshire, but it's not certain that his relics were there at the time of Germanus' visit, nor that he underwent martyrdom there. Perhaps Germanus' reason for visiting the place was to give the seal of approval to the adoration of relics, and the marking of a martyr or saint's burial place by the erection of a church: practices which were becoming popular on the Continent at that time. A small church was built above St Martin's grave in 397, soon after his burial. If Germanus did bring and take relics, such an act would have forged a stronger link between the Church in Britain and in continental Europe.

St Albans church is sited on a Roman cemetery, and it's unusual that memories concerning the martyr, and respect towards him, should have survived the pagan Saxon onslaught even to this day, when all recollection of any other, similar sites has been lost. The native Britons must have been able to stand their ground thereabouts, and the lack of Anglo-Saxon remains in the area from before the end of the seventh century is testimony to that effect. Archaeological evidence indicates that the place was in pretty dire condition by c.350 AD, but also that buildings were still being repaired and erected in the Roman city and on nearby hills during the fifth century.

Constantius seems to presuppose his Gaulish readers know of Alban, and it appears that several old churches in Germany, including some important foundations in the Rhine Valley such as Albansberg (Mainz) were consecrated in his name. Alban is also mentioned in a poem by Venantius Fortunatus, Bishop of Poitiers (died *c.*600 AD).

More of Alban the Martyr is found in Gildas' *De Excidio Britanniae* (On the Destruction of Britain), and Bede's *Historia Ecclesiastica gentes Anglorum* (Ecclesiastical History of the English People). Sharpe's theory is that all these reports derive from a single early record, the *Passio Albani*. The earliest copy of that document (Text "T") is in Turin in Italy, and dates from the eighth century: but is based on an older text. It reports, amongst other things, that Alban appeared to Germanus during his journey to Britain, revealing in a dream the means of his martyrdom. The bishop then "made this public, so that the incidents could be recorded in writing on wall-hangings." If used by Gildas, the *Passio* must have been composed between 429 (the year of Germanus' visit) and the mid-sixth century (the time *De Excidio* was written).

Another ancient text of the *Passio* ("E"), states as follows:

"When St Germanus came to Alban's basilica, bringing with him relics of all the apostles and several martyrs, he ordered that the grave be opened for him so that valuable gifts could be put in the same place, so that the single grave would contain the members of saints brought from various places...he took from the place where the martyr's blood flowed a piece of soil in which it could be seen that the earth was red with blood remaining since the martyr's death..."

Sharpe maintains that there is evidence that the *Passio* could be older than Constantius' work (c.480), and perhaps followed the writing (in paint) of the story of Alban's life and passion on wooden boards at Germanus' command before his death (in 446, according to Sharpe). A document written in Auxerre in the ninth century (the *Gesta episcoporum Autissiodorensium*) states that St Germanus founded "the basilica of Saint Alban within the walls of Auxerre, which he consecrated in honour of the martyr, and honourably placed there the relics which he brought with him from Britain". We may accept, therefore, that Alban was a subject of interrest in Auxerre at that time; that a church in Alban's name was to be found there, and that it was believed that relics of Alban rested there. Is this where the wall-hangings were to be seen?

(Regarding the placing of relics in Alban's grave, see Chapter 2).

13) See Sulpicius Severus' *Letter to Eusebius* for a similar incident from the life of St Martin.

14) Archbishop James Ussher (1591 – 1656) in his *Britannicarum Ecclesiarum Antiquitates* ... (Dublin 1639) is the first to name Maes Garmon near Mold as the site of Germanus and the Britons' victory on Easter Sunday, 430 AD (see Chapter 6). This has been doubted, as the tradition is comparatively late, and the topography thereabouts is not mountainous: nevertheless, the battle's reputed site is marked by an obelisk raised in 1736 by Nehemiah Griffith of Rhual (see Chapter 8). Other suggested sites of the battle include Bwlch yr Oernant (the "Horseshoe Pass") near Llanarmon yn Iâl; the Chilterms, as the story of the battle follows that of the visit to St Albans; Derbyshire; the Humber, and north Kent. In light of St Germanus' connections with the Kingdom of Powys, it has been suggested that he had a leading rôle in restoring the control of the regional centre at Wroxeter over the uplands of present-day north Powys.

It has been doubted that this battle ever took place. Blair, for instance, suggests it to be "no more than a tale conceived by someone who had misunderstood the whole situation and supposed that Germanus' victory had been won in a military battle rather than a theological argument". In

41

support of the veracity of Constantius' account, however, is the possibility that Germanus had performed military duties, and Constantius' use of the term *sagulum* (i.e. general's cloak) to describe the mantle under which the saint used to sleep. Constantius' description of Germanus' tactics in fighting the enemy (forming a camp; staging a raid; not using the entire army at one time; making the best of the topography, and not cornering the enemy) are entirely consistent with contemporary Roman military practice. The description of the enemy's advance along one path and their subsequent flight in all directions may echo Deuteronomy 28:7, and the loud shouts are reminiscent of Joshua 6:1-20, and 2 Chronicles 13:15-17.

Regarding the baptism of soldiers before battle: the testimony of Blessèd Augustine and other authors of that period is that some would delay baptism (and so, in their view, the complete forgiveness of their sins) until the last moment before death (see Chapter 4). Wood suspects that the battle is largely allegorical (see Chapter 2).

15) Arles (Arelate), between Montpellier and Marseilles in Provence, was at that time the capital of the Diocese of Gaul, i.e. that westernmost part of the Empire stretching from Morocco to Britain.

16) Alise-Sainte-Reine (Alesia), 20 miles north-west of Dijon in Burgundy.

17) See Chapter 8 of Sulpicius Severus' *Second Dialogue concerning Saint Martin* for a similar incident.

18) Lyons (Lugudunum) stands where the Saône flows into the Rhône, about half way between Auxerre and Arles. Between 178 and 200 this was the home of the renowned theologian, St Irenaeus. Eucherius was Bishop of Lyons at the time of Germanus' visit: he too had been forced to accept the post by popular acclaim. He died about the year 449/450, having performed his duties for twenty years. Much more may be learnt of him in Chadwick (1955): St John Cassian dedicated the second part of his *Conferences* to Honoratus and Eucherius of Lérins (see Chapter 4).

19) Saint Hilarius, Metropolitan of Arles, and leader of the Church in Gaul 429-449. The *Vita S. Hilarii Arelatensis* by Reverentius (c.500) states that Hilarius used to seek and receive Germanus' opinion, which suggests that the Bishop of Auxerre was in high regard among his Gaulish bretheren. Reverentius states that Germanus advised Hilarius regarding accusations against Chelidonius, Bishop of Besançon, who was dethroned in 444. This does not necessarily mean that Germanus was still alive at that time, for such cases tended to drag on for years. It's possible that Hilarius conferred with Germanus during the latter's visit to Ravenna in 437, or that Reverentius brought Germanus' name into his account of the proceedings in order to give a better gloss to Hilarius' highly controversial actions.

In Wales, the church at Rogiet in Monmouthshire was anciently dedicated in his name. Not so Llanilar and Eglwys Rhos, which were consecrated in the name of St Hilary of Poitiers.

20) According to Bede, and he alone, this Bishop Severus was that Severus (+476) who had been one of Lupus' disciples, and was made Bishop of Trier in 446. Some scholars have attempted to link this second visit with Gildas' report that the Britons had appealed in vain to Aëtius (see note 22 below) for aid against the Saxons about the period 446 - 454, and the revival of Pelagianism with a reaction against the Romans: but there is good evidence for 437 as the date of the second visit. In addition to that evidence, the present writer draws attention to Bede's exact words, to wit that Severus was "a particularly holy man, and afterwards as Bishop of Trier." *And afterwards* as Bishop of Trier: if he was ordained bishop in 446, then the suggestion is that the second visit to Britian took place before then. No list of bishops of Trier exists for this period, and Levison posits that Constantius' "Bishop Severus" may have been Severus of Vence (in Provence), present at the Synods of Riez (439) and Vaison (442).

Though Rome lost (or released) Britain by 410, it did not follow that Roman control would not be re-imposed once circumstances allowed. The Emperor Constantius had restored Roman rule here by defeating Allectus in 296, and likewise Stilicho in 398-400, following the revolt of Magnus

Maximus (383).

Trier (Augusta Treverorum) stands a little east of Luxembourg. It was capital of the western Empire for a time at the end of the third century and the begining of the fourth, and then capital of the province of Gaul. Following the removal of the imperial capital to Milan and the regional capital to Arles, in went into decline. The birthplace of St Ambrose (see note 25 below).

21) To where on the continent were these Pelagians exiled? Gaul, or Italy, perhaps? Chapter 51 of Sulpicius Severus' *Sacred History* records the exile of the Priscillian heretic bishops Instantius and Tiberianus from Aquitaine to "the island of Sylina...beyond Britain" in 384, i.e. the Scilly Isles, in all probability.

22) Saxon settlers seem to have arrived in Kent in the 420's, and according to the *Gaulish Chronicle of 452* began their revolt against Vortigern about the year 441/2. Ten years of fierce fighting followed, until Vortimer (Vortigern's son) won victory at Richborough about the year 450. This record may indicate political instability in south-eastern Britain at about that time, even if Dark is correct in proposing that the Saxons did not arrive en masse until about 450, and did not revolt until c.490/500.

Wherever and whenever Germanus visited Britain, public order was such that he could travel and preach safely, and ensure the exiling of heretics. That would be possible in south-west and south-east Britain in 429, and even in 437: but perhaps not in Kent in the year 448, if that was the place and date of the second visit. Constantius' information about this point is quite hazy, and some have doubted there was a second visit: but the definite naming of Elafius as one with authority "in those parts" suggests that the report has some foundation.

Wade-Evans (1920) and others have speculated that this Elafius was none other than Elesa, alleged founder of the Anglo-Saxon dynasty of Wessex. This would place the incident in the Hampshire area, west of Kent. It's a tempting theory, as Elesa's supposed immediate descendants, rulers such as Cerdic, Cynric and others, have suspiciously Brittonic-sounding names, not Saxon ones: and it has been mooted that they were, in fact, native British rulers subsequently grafted onto a royal Anglo-Saxon family tree, to lend it legitimacy (see Russell, M., in Bibliography). Cerdic, however, is thought to have reigned about the early to mid-sixth century: rather too late for his predecessor to have been the magnate who met Germanus, even if the latter's second visit took place in 448 AD.

23) The general Aëtius, *magister militium* of Gaul and a German by descent, came to the fore as a powerful governor in the year 425, and by 437 was virtual ruler of the western Empire. He succeeded in halting Attila the Hun in Gaul in 451, and again in

Italy the following year. If at any time afterwards he envisaged re-establishing Roman rule in Britain, nothing came of it: for in 455 he was accused of treason (having yielded much territory to the Goths and Burgundians), and executed by order of Valentinian III (see note 28 below).

First mention of the Alans comes from Roman sources of the 1st century AD, as a fierce, nomadic tribe dwelling north of the Caucasus. Of Iranian descent, they were defeated by the Huns in 370, and fled westwards, eventually combining with the Vandals and Swabians and pouring into Gaul in 406. The pretender Constantine III led an army from Britain against them, forcing most to flee again, southwards this time. On the way to Spain, the Swabians turned against the Alans, destroying them. It's probable that any remainder joined the Vandals, crossing into north Africa in 429.

However, some Alans remained in the Orléans - Vienne area of Gaul, employed by the Romans on policing duties in Armorica. Settling there and being absorbed into the aristocracy, the name "Alain/Alan" acquired high status, and remains a popular Christian name in Brittany (and beyond) to this day. Goar is mentioned in Gregory of Tours' *Decem Libri Historianum*, and is likely to have first arrived in those parts about the year 406. That being so, his career as leader would have been more likely to last until the 430s than the 440s (see note 32 below). Similarly, Aëtius employed Visigoths to put down a popular rebellion in northern Spain in 454.

Apart from the possibility that Germanus was once governor of Armorica, the rebels' readiness to appeal to him is an example of ecclesiastical leaders of that period having to shoulder legal and judicial duties. St Paul, of course, encourages Christians to settle differences amongst themselves (I Corinthians 6:1-6): but by Germanus' day, as civil order in the western Empire collapsed, there was an increasing tendency for bishops to perform both ecclesiastical and secular functions, the Church being virtually the sole organized functioning entity. Public office had ceased to be an honour (*honor*), and had become a financial burden (*muneo*): and as local oligarchs shunned centres of population and administrative responsibilities in favour of safeguarding their own rural estates, the Roman authorities were only too ready to place the burden on anyone remotely capable. St Patrick informs us that his father held offices both sacred (deacon) and profane (decurion). This process facilitated the adoption by western Christianity of Roman legalistic appearances, forms and attitudes, reflecting the same in its theology.

24) Ravenna on the shores of the Adriatic was capital – and most flourishing city – of the western Empire since Honorius moved his court there from Milan in 402. Its port was the chief point of contact with eastern parts of the Empire. Landward, the city was surrounded by swamps

defensive, but malarial.

25) Autun in the south of France, the Roman Augustodunum.

26) Milan, the Roman Mediolanum. An important centre which had been capital of the western Empire during the fourth century, before Ravenna took the crown. The city is associated with Saint Ambrose (c.339 – 397), excellent preacher, immoveable prop of Catholicism, and defender of the Church. Despite some uncertainty in the text at this point, it's likely that the "saints" referred to are the patron saints of Milan, Gervasius and Protasius. Their feast was kept on the 19th of June. Bearing in mind that St Ambrose's father was one Aurelius Ambrosius, it's possible that he was related to the Ambrosius Aurelianus named by Nennius as leader of the Britons (see *Historia Brittonum* 48 in Chapter 3 of this work, and note 7 in that same chapter). However, that leader may himself have been named after this well-known saint (see Chapter 3). Blessèd Augustine supplies further information about Saint Ambrose in Book IX of his *Confessions*.

27) One could live – very modestly - on the equivalent of two gold pieces per annum. With admirable precision, E.O. Williams, writing in 1857, declares a golden solidus to be "these days worth 17s. 8d."

28) St Peter Chrysologus ("the golden word"), c.400 –

450. "The Empress" was Galla Placidia (c.390 – 450), daughter of Theodosius the Great (who defeated Magnus Maximus), and Honorius' half-sister. Her adventurous life and the many perils she had faced had instilled in her a forceful personality, and she dominated her son Valentinian III ("the Emperor"). Her mausoleum at Ravenna contains some of that period's most splendid mosaics. Valentinian III reigned from 425 to 455. He is known to have been in Ravenna to greet Germanus, but afterwards no mention is made of him until arrangements are made to bear the saint's relics homewards shortly after the 25th of July. As he is also known to have sailed from Rome to Constantinople on the 15th of July 437 in order to marry Eudoxia, then either the year of Germanus' mission could not have been 437, or the said arrangements were made in the Emperor's name, not by Valentinian himself. He was eventually murdered in Rome by Aëtius' supporters, in revenge for that general's execution.

29) Letters of St Paulinus of Nola record his sending similar gifts to his friends, including loaves and a wooden platter to Sulpicius Severus. Like the Empress, the recipients could hardly have stood in need of such items, so one may presume that such basic necessities were symbolic of the giver's sustaining affection.

30) A very similar story appears in the *Life of St Columbanus* by Jonas of Bobbio, c.643 AD.

31) See I Kings 17:21, II Kings 4:34, 35, and Acts 20:10.

Also Sulpicius Severus' *Life of St Martin*, Chapters 7 and 8. Sigisvult is first mentioned in 429, and was consul by 437. Constantius gives him the title *patricius*, which would have been improbable before 440, unless Germanus' biographer is mistaken (see note 33 below).

32) Zosimus in his *Historia Nova* mentions a rebellion in Armorica shortly after 409. The resulting chaos may have lasted a considerable time, despite a defeat of the rebels by Exuperantius in 417 (see Chapter 4, note 24). Tibatto's rebellion broke out there in 435, and is probably the one Constantius had in mind. The *Gaulish Chronicle of 452* states that it was quashed by Litorus in 437.

Memories of this Armorican rebellion may, perhaps, be incorporated in the *Life of Holy King Solomon of Brittany* by Paulilianus of Léon (10th century). He writes of the murder of the king by rebels, who were then defeated by Valentinian's forces.

33) According to the *Life of Amator (Vita Amatoris)*, Germanus died on Sunday, May the 26th. According to two later sources, *Martyrologium Hieronymianum* and *De Gestis episcoporum Autissiodorensium*, he died on July the 31st. The latter also states that Germanus was bishop for thirty-five years and twenty-five days. According to his biography, Amator died on Wednesday the 1st of May, and therefore in either

407, 412 or 418 AD. Given that, we can deduce that Germanus visited Britain for the second time in either 437, 442 or 448 AD. The *Vita Seueri* states clearly that Germanus' relics were borne through Vienne on their way from Ravenna to Auxerre before the 8th of November 441. Most scholars favour the period 445-448, but Thompson has compelling arguments in favour of 437. Wood favours either 437 or 442, but definitely not 448.

34) Piacenza, the Roman Placentio, 130 miles from Ravenna.

35) The practice of healing by sleeping under or on a shrine or reliquary ("incubation") became very widespread.

36) Germanus' remains were buried in the monastery founded by him (see note 6 above). Sometime before 545 they were translated to an abbey built at saintly Queen Clotilda's command for the express purpose of housing them. A monastic community is mentioned there about the year 725: it adopted the Rule of St Benedict in 817. About the year 840 Conrad, uncle of King Charles the Bald, was miraculously healed before Germanus' relics, and vowed to build a new church wherein the saint's remains could be displayed. On the 28th of August 841, the day of their translation thence, the tomb was opened in Charles' presence, and the relics found to be incorrupt. Charles ordered them wrapped in silks. The relics were translated again on the 6th of January 859, down to a crypt ordered

made by Conrad for that sole purpose. It is known that Hugh, Bishop of Châlons donated silk patterned with eagles for the wrapping of the relics in 1030.

When Auxerre was seized by the Huguenots in 1567, the relics were flung away. It is said that they were collected and subsequently housed at the Abbey of Saint-Marion (Saint Marianus, see note 6 above), but the authenticity of those remains is not widely accepted. The abbey was confiscated during the French Revolution of 1789, and the clergy's belongings sold two years later. The western part of the abbey was demolished in order to create a hospital entrance in 1811.

There remains the tomb, and pieces of a purple silk wrapping patterned with golden eagles. It was woven in Constantinople about the year 1000, and originally seems to have been a chasuble: but the pattern thereon does not match exactly the description of Bishop Hugh's gift. A fragment may be seen in Evans and Wixon, pp.224-225 (see Bibliography).

The remains of Saint Germanus' fortified abbey (Saint-Germain) stand in Auxerre to this day, being mainly a tower and part of a high wall. It is now a museum.

2. The "Life": a History

The first notices of St Germanus are found in the *Gaulish Chronicle of 452*, where under the year 433 it is stated that "Germanus, the Bishop of Auxerre, is illustrious for his virtues and for the austerity of his life". Prosper Tiro's *Epitoma Chronicon* states under the year 429 that "The Pelagian Agricola, son of the Pelagian bishop Severianus, corrupts the churches of Britain by the introduction of his doctrine; but at the suggestion of the deacon Palladius, Pope Celestine sends Germanus, bishop of Auxerre, as his own representative, and after the overthrow of the heretics, guides the Britons to the Catholic faith."

The *Life* of St Germanus was composed by the venerable Constantius of Lyons sometime about 475 – 480, at the request of Patiens, bishop of that city c.449\451 - 491. Having been a short time in circulation in Lyons, it was published at the request of Censurius, Bishop of Auxerre 472-502. Constantius dedicated the *Life* to these two bishops, and implied in a prefatory letter that some time had passed since Germanus' death. Over a hundred manuscripts of it are known, dating from the eighth century onwards. We don't know exactly why it was written, but Constantius was probably aware of the value of an exemplar of episcopal behaviour, which could also inspire and give heart to these bishops and their flocks in the face of Burgundian assaults. He may also have been eager to reinforce the archbishopric of Lyons against the growing prestige of that of Tours.[1]

Constantius was a monk, and perhaps a priest, of noble lineage, a fine orator and a good poet. His friend, the author Sidonius Apollinaris (c.430 – 480, a rich landowner who became a *praefectus urbi*, and subsequently Bishop of Clermont-Ferrand about the year 470), had a high opinion of his literary abilities. His compact, clear, lively style is evidence of thorough training. He was born in Lyons c.415, and spent his life there. He valiantly aided Sidonius in the defence of Clermont-Ferrand against the Visigoths in 473.

His *Vita S. Germani* is founded upon two immensely influential works, the *Life of St Anthony* by St Athanasius (357) and the *Life of St Martin, Bishop of Tours* by Sulpicius Severus (c.397). Prior to the publication of these works, Christians drew comfort and learning from the acts of the martyrs: but with the cessation of official persecution, and the rise of monasticism as a contemporary means of abandoning all in order to follow Christ, a need arose for a new kind of literature recording and encouraging imitation of the works of spiritual heroes in their perpetual battle against the forces of evil.

Constantius set about composing a "life", not a "report". Neither he nor his audience were much interested in historical detail, unless it reflected the subject's sanctity and depicted the makings of an ideal bishop. However, he gives accurate details regarding Germanus' life on the Continent, including the names of important personages and their functions, even at Ravenna. Less sure is his grasp on the visits to Britain, especially the second visit. This has led some to suspect the latter of being but a literary device or error on the part of author, or the conflation of two different accounts of a single visit. However, the inclusion of Elafius' name and "title", rather than a vague reference to an additional miracle, seems to record a definite, separate incident.

One gets the impression that Constantius, writing of visits to Britain half a century before, is using second-hand information about a place of which he had not much knowledge. By 480 the Jutes and Saxons had begun settling in numbers in the very areas, perhaps, were Germanus had been active, and all native testimony may have been dispersed. Yet Constantius worked at the fringes of living memory, and Lupus (who was also in touch with Sidonius Apollinaris) may have lived long enough to provide him with information. So despite the lack of detail in places, it would have been difficult to include in the work anything known, remembered or suspected by his audience of being untrue.[2]

Regarding the unrest in Armorica, Constantius' attitude reflects that of his own kin and the social status of his audience. He has sympathy with neither rebels nor rebellion. The rebels, on the other hand, seek Germanus' aid: they believe he understands their aims and motives, and that he is merciful, even sympathetic. This is additional information for believing that the bishop may, at one time, have been Governor of Armorica, and that the rebels knew from experience that he could be appealed to successfully in the face of oppression.

Saint Isidore of Seville (570-636) in his *De Vitis Illustrium Virorum* states: *"Constantius episcopus Germani vitam contexit"*, i.e. "Bishop Constantius made the Life of Germanus". He may have been under the impression that Constantius was a bishop, or *episcopus* may be in mistake for *episcopi*, which would give "Constantius made the Life of Bishop Germanus".

Some remains of Constantius' text, dating from the 8th century, are contained in manucript Bibl-Nat., Paris, Nouvelles Acq., Lat.12,598. This was printed by the Abbé Narbey in his *Etude critique sur la vie de S.Germain*, Paris 1884. It contains quotations from a fuller copy of the *Life*, for use in a church, mainly those parts concerning Germanus' humility.

Sometime about 573 – 589 Bishop Aunarius of Auxerre asked Stephanus Africanus to compose a *Life of St Germanus* in verse. If composed, it has not survived: but about 864-5 Abbot Lothair of St Germain in Auxerre found a copy of Aunarius' letter, and asked the monk Heiric (c.835 – 887) to undertake the task.

It says much of Auxerre's pre-eminence at that time that its abbot was a son of King Charles the Bald, then Western Europe's foremost cultural patron. The publication of the *Life* and *Miracles* would have increased the abbey's prestige, especially when compared to the rival abbey of Tours. It could also have been commissioned with an eye to increasing the lucrative flow of pilgrims from the British Isles, where St Germanus was well-known. By about 873-5 Heiric of Auxerre had composed a *Life* in six books of hexameters, and a prose *Miracula sancti Germani*.[3] In the eighth chapter of the first book of the *Miracula* (see Migne, *Patrologia Latina* 124, col. 1245-6), is recorded a tale very similar to the miracle of the calf found in Nennius' work (see Chapter 3).

Heiric says that he heard the story from an elder named Marcus, a Welsh bishop who had been educated in Ireland, and had come to France on pilgrimage. He was living as a hermit in Soissons, and much famed for his sanctity (*singularis nostro tempore unicae philosophus sanctitatis*). He often told the tale, and swore to Heiric that it was to be found in Britain "in catholic letters" (*catholicis litteris*): a Latin religious book, perhaps. Was Marcus referring to Nennius' work, or had he seen a manuscript similar to the one mentioned by Nennius as one of his sources, the *Book of Blessèd Germanus*?[4]

By the end of the 6th century, the Life of Germanus had accumulated additions not found in Constantius' original, but were later supposed to be true elements of the Life, viz:

a) Germanus when a layman was fond of hunting, and would hang trophies of the chase on a tree, after the manner of a pagan sacrifice. St Amator, Bishop of Auxerre, felled the tree, and ordained Germanus priest. The death of Amator, and the miracle which followed. These details derived from the *Life of St Amator* by Stephanus Africanus, written at the request of Aunarius (Aunachar), Bishop of Auxerre 573-603.[5]

b) The conversion of Mamertinus at the grave of Corcodemus.

c) The colloquy of Geneviève and Germanus at Nanterre, as he journeyed to Britain the first time; and the intervention of Germanus on Geneviève's behalf on his way to Britain a second time (see Chapter 5).

d) Germanus seeks, finds and translates the relics of St Alban. Germanus leaves relics of all the apostles and of several martyrs in St Alban's tomb.

e) The revelation of the day of Julian's martyrdom, when Germanus visited Brioude.

f) Germanus' visit to St John Cassian's grave at Autun, and his conversation with the dead man.

g) Comments upon St Germanus' carrying a lame man on his shoulders across an Alpine river.

A version of the *Life of St Gernamus* was published by Mombritius in Milan in 1480, in the first volume of his *Sanctuarium*. The foreword and conclusion were excluded, but a late addition included, viz. a tale of Germanus bringing to life a dead donkey. It does not include the dedicatory passages, but the superscript "Constantius ad Patiens episcopum..." indicates that the copy Mombritius used contained such a dedication.

The version containing additions a – g above was published by Laurentius Surius (1522-78) in his *De probatis Sanctorum historiis* (Cologne 1570-75). Due to the additions' stress on the miraculous and wondrous, later commentators (e.g. Krusch in *Passiones vitaeque sanctorum aevi merovingici*, and Schoel in *De Ecclesiasticae Britonum Scotorumque Historiae Fontibus*) supposed that the whole *Life of Germanus* was but fantasy. Thereafter, however, scholars such as Sabine Baring-Gould drew attention to the manuscript Bibl-Nat., Paris, Nouvelles Acq., Lat.2178. This had been written in Silos, Spain, in the 12th century, copying a document sufficiently early not to contain the above accretions.

The standard text was edited by Wilhelm Levison in his *Monumenta Germaniae Historica, Scriprotum Rerum Merovingicarum*, vol. VII, pp. 247-283, 1920. This was translated into English by F. R. Hoare for his *The Western Fathers* (New York, n.d.), and the work you are now reading is based on Hoare's text.

The Life of St Germanus: an allegory?

In his important article *The End of Roman Britain: Continental Evidence and Parallels* (1984), Ian Wood argues that Constantius' *Life of St Germanus* should be understood as an allegory, not an historical account. The purpose of the work, he says, was to provide an example of inspired leadership for contemporary bishops such as Patiens of Lyons who were facing pagan invasions and the rise of heresies.

According to Wood, the first part of the Life removes Germanus from the secular sphere to the sacred by a progressive series of exorcisms. Beginning as a secular officer (with the suggestion that he had been a regional governor), he proceeds as priest to display his sacred authority over the "official" world in the case of the tax collector; over the world "at large" in the case of the plague-stricken people of Auxerre; over the church in the case of the prophetic monk; over the dead in the case of the buried robbers, and over nature in the case of the mute cockerels. The extent and depth of a faith-inspired bishop's ability is revealed step by step.

Wood has it that the visits to Britain, and subsequently Arles and Ravenna, also contain strong allegorical elements which tend to disregard to saint's lack of success. The miracle of the unburnt house illustrates the importance of complete subjection to God's will in order to ensure safety, in contrast to the Pelagians' stress on free will. Similar "fiery" miracles may be found in "lives" of other Gaulish saints, i.e. Martin, Eutropius and Caesarius. The restoration of the blind girl's sight could be interpreted as the reillumination of Britain after ten years of Pelagianism (i.e. the period between the interdict of 418 and Germanus' first visit in 429), and so also the healing of Elafius' son during the second visit.

The allegory continues with the Hallelujah Battle. The incident starts during Lent, the proper canonical period of preparation for Easter, i.e. the feast reserved for the sacrament of baptism. Having baptised the soldiers, a battle takes place at which Catholic Christianity trounces enemy arms, without one drop of blood staining either the bishop or the newly-baptised.

In reading the *Life of Saint Germanus*, says Wood, one should bear in mind Patiens in Lyons facing the might of the Burgundians, or Constantius himself travelling to raise the spirits of the people of Clermont, rather than concentrate attention primarily on British history. Constantius' main message is probably that a bishop's duty is to provide his flock with spiritual arms: God will provide the security. That's why the first part of the *Life of Saint Germanus* stresses faith and divine aid, not good works. This is underlined by the relation between true faith and bodily health.

Wood does not deny that Constantius' work contains historical elements, but goes further than other scholars in stressing the allegorical content. Thus he seeks to underline the differences between Constantius' thought, attitude and purposes in the fifth century and those of the historians and biographers of western European secular culture at the turn of the twenty-first century.

J. K. Knight's standpoint is similar. Supporting Wood, he holds that Constantius' intention was to compare Germanus to a prophet, an apostle or even to Christ himself, recording, borrowing or devising "facts" to that end. So he could not state that Germanus had sailed to Britain, for instance, without losing an opportunity to depict him imitating Christ's miracle of the calming of the Sea of Galilee. Apart from the Bible, Constantius could also draw on Classical sources, as when he transplants the tale of the haunted ruin from the works of Pliny (*Letters* VII, 27). Where Constantius saw need of filling any gaps in the narrative, he expanded on his own knowledge. Thus he mentions Picts and Saxons in the context of the Hallelujah Battle, for instance, because he understood that Germanus had taken the field, and that those peoples were attacking Britain at that time.[6] In fact, Constantius didn't know who'd been defeated, and didn't much care: it was enough to record that Germanus was victor.

In the glare of hypercriticism, any text originating in the distant past can be so deconstructed as to be reduced to a point at which nothing tangible of it remains. An attempt to peel away that which seems to us subjective, illogical, or poorly attested, in order to uncover a core of indisputable, objective "fact", may be doomed from the outset by the paucity of such "hard evidence" as remains 1,600 years after the events in question. We end up throwing away both oyster and pearl.

In the case of the *Life of St Germanus*, the present writer believes that Constantius' account contains a kernel of Truth. There was a Bishop of Auxerre named Germanus; he was an exceptional man of his age; visited both Britain and Ravenna, and was much regarded by a wide range of his contemporaries for his humility, diplomacy, faith and leadership. Faith dictates what else we may believe concerning this remarkable man of God.

Notes

1. In writing of Germanus, a heroic, cultured Gaulish nobleman (and perhaps pointedly unlike Martin of Tours), Constantius may also have been attempting to counter the growing tendency to appoint monastic bishops to Gaulish sees, rather than local aristocrats. This would have been in line with contemporary papal policy. N. K. Chadwick (1950) regards the spread of Martin dedications to England and Scotland as a product of rivalry between Tours and Auxerre/Lyons. See also Chapter 7.

2. The rôle, career and character of Lupus of Troyes are further discussed by N. K. Chadwick (1955). Sources other than Constantius link Lupus with Germanus: and the fact that the sees of Auxerre and Troyes are adjacent cannot fully account for this coupling. Sidonius Apollinaris praises Lupus

as the most eminent Gaulish bishop of that time, but it remains unclear why he should do so, if not for some great feat such as the mission to Britain.

3. Heiric names Germanus' parents as Rusticus and Germanilla, stating that they were buried in a church dedicated in the name of St Peter, on their own estate at Epponiacus.

4. More of Bishop Marcus, and his possible connections with Rome, St Gall, Ireland and the court of Rhodri Mawr in Gwynedd, can be found in N. K. Chadwick (1958(a)). She concludes that "It would seem that he was the principal authority on St Germanus in French intellectual circles in the ninth century."

5. As E. O. Williams relates:
"He [Germanus] possessed a large estate, and found amusement in hunting. After each day's sport he used to hang the heads of the beasts he had slain on a pine-tree in the town of Auxerre, until Amator, bishop of that see, caused this tree to be cut down. Garmon vowed revenge; but, before he put his threat into execution, the bishop was warned in a vision that his death was nigh, and that he who threatened him would succeed him in his bishopric. Accordingly he seized Garmon, and ordained him deacon. When Garmon recovered from his astonishment, 'God who had directed the whole affair, so touched his heart, that upon the death of Amator, a few days afterwards, he was chosen to succeed him, and made his life a model

of the episcopal character.' In allusion to this legend St. Garmon is represented as a bishop, with dead or hunted beasts lying around him."

More of Amator may be found in N. K. Chadwick (1955), who detects a kernel of truth in Africanus' account.

6. Constantius, however, may have had in mind Ammianus Marcellinus' account of the "Barbarian Conspiracy", which describes the co-ordinated, simultaneous attack of Picts, Saxons and other peoples on Britain in the year 367. Had there been a similar operation in St Germanus' time, it would not have been without precedent.

3. Nennius

The author (or authors) known as Nennius probably wrote the *Historia Brittonum* ("History of the Britons") in Gwynedd, about the period 796 - 801. It was composed at the behest of Elfoddw, Bishop of Bangor, who is known to have brought the Church in north Wales into line with current Anglo-Roman practice. The *Historia* could have been commissioned to draw parallels between this feat and Germanus' exploit in bringing Britain into religious conformity with Rome four hundred years previously. It is also a masterly work of propaganda on behalf of the rulers of Gwynedd *contra* those of neighbouring Powys.

It relates the story of how a ruler entitled Vortigern ("Great King") lost control over Britain to Teutonic mercenaries. It contains the following references to St Germanus, listed here according to the chapter numbers of the original work.

32. In his [Vortigern's] time holy Germanus came to preach in Britain, and became famous in their midst because of his many abilities, and through him many were saved, though many went to perdition.[1]

I decided that some of the miracles God wrought through him should be recorded.

The first miracle.

There was an evil king named Benlli, a great oppressor. The holy man [Germanus] wished to visit him, and hurried to preach to the evil ruler. But when the man of God and his companions came to the city gate, a doorkeeper greeted them, and they sent him to the king: and the king answered coarsely with an oath, saying "Even if they're here, and wait here until the year's end, they'll never be admitted to my city". As they waited for the doorkeeper to bring them the king's message, it grew late, and began to get dark, and they knew not where to go. Then one of the king's servants came out of the city, and bowed before the man of God, repeating to him the king's words: and he invited them to stay in his own house. They went out with him, and he welcomed them. But he had no animals of any kind, but a cow and calf, and he killed the calf, and cooked it, and put it before them. But holy Germanus commanded that no bone of it should be broken: and so it was, and the following morning the calf was found with its mother, healthy, alive and uninjured.[2]

33. They arose early, and again attempted to address the king. But as they prayed and waited outside the fortress gate, behold a man running towards them, with sweat dripping from the crown of his head to the soles of his feet. He bowed before them, and holy Germanus said "Do you believe in the Holy Trinity?", and he replied "I believe". And he was baptized. He kissed him, and said "Go in peace. Within the hour you will die, and God's angels are awaiting you in heaven, any you will go with them to God, in Whom you believe." He

went joyfully into the fort, and the official caught him, and bound him, and he was led before the king and slain, for it was the loathsome ruler's custom that anyone who did not reach the fort before sunrise to serve him should be killed. They stayed by the city gate all day, but did not succeed in addressing the king.

34. The abovementioned servant was there, as usual, and holy Germanus said to him "Beware lest any of your men stay in this fort tonight." So he returned to the fort and brought out his sons, nine in number, and they returned with him to the aforesaid lodging. Saint Germanus told them to remain fasting behind closed doors, saying "Be watchful, and should anything happen in the fort, do not look, but continue in prayer and to call upon your God ceaselessly." Shortly, fire fell from heaven, and burnt the fort and all the men who were with the king, and to this day no sign of them has been seen of them, and to this day the fort has not been rebuilt.[3]

35. The following morning, the man who sheltered them believed and was baptized with all his sons, and the whole area along with them. His name was Cadell. Germanus blessed him, and in addition said "From your seed a king will never be wanting (for Cadell Ddyrnllwg is he), and you only will be king from henceforth." So it was, and thus were the words of the prophet fulfilled: "He raiseth up the poor out of the dust, and lifteth up the beggar out of the dung-hill, to set them among

princes, and to make them inherit the throne of glory:"⁴ In accordance with St Germanus' words, from a servant he was made a king, and all his sons were made kings, and from their seed is ruled the entire land of Powys, to this day….

39. Then, in addition to all his wrongdoings, Vortigern took his own daughter as wife, and had a child by her. When this was made known to holy Germanus, he came with all the clerics of Britain to accuse him. When the great Synod of clerics and laymen came together as one council, the king told his daughter beforehand to come to the meeting, and place her son on Germanus' lap, and say thay he [Germanus] was the child's father. The woman did as she was ordered, but Germanus received the child kindly, and said to him "I'll be a father to you, and won't send you away, unless a razor and scissors and comb are given to me, and it is permitted that you give them to your father according to the flesh."⁵ The boy heard him, and turned to Vortigern his father, and said to him "You are my father. Shave my head, and the hair of my head." But he was silent, and said nothing, and refused to answer the child. He arose in great wrath, and fled from before the face of holy Germanus, and was accursed, and he was condemned by holy Germanus and the entire assembly of the Britons…

44. …but Vortimer died shortly afterwards. Before he died, he asked his followers to dig his grave by the coast, at the port from which they [the Saxons] had

left, saying "I entrust it to you. Wherever they occupy a British port or gain a foothold, they'll never live here again." But they ignored his order and did not bury him where he told them: for he was buried in Lincoln. But if they had obeyed him, they would without doubt have had whatever they wished by the prayers of holy Germanus.[6]

47. But holy Germanus preached to Vortigern, to turn him to his Lord, and dissolve his illegal union. But he fled in despair to the land called Gwrtheyrnion after him, and hid there with his wives. So holy Germanus followed him there with all the clerics of Britain, and stayed there forty days and forty nights, standing day and night on a stone, addressing him. Then Vortigern retreated in shame to Caer Gwrtheyrn, in the land of the men of Dyfed, on the Teifi.[7] Holy Germanus followed him as before, and stayed there fasting with the clerics for three days and as many nights in order to succeed in his purpose, and on the fourth night, about midnight, the entire fort was suddenly destroyed by fire sent from heaven, and the heavenly fire burnt: Vortigern, and all those with him, and with all his wives, were destroyed. That was the end of Vortigern, as I found it in the book of the blessèd Germanus; but others have other versions.[8]

48. He [Vortigern] had three sons, and their names are Vortimer, who fought against the barbarians, as I have described above; the second, Cateyrn; the third, Pascen, who ruled in the two lands called

Buallt and Gwrtheyrnion following his father's death, by permission of Ambrosius, who was a great king amongst all the kings of the British nation. Faustus was a fourth son, born to him of his daughter. Holy Germanus baptized him, and raised him, and educated him, and he founded a monastery on the banks of a river, named Renis, which stands to this day...[9]

49. Here is his pedigree, which goes back to his family. Farinmail himself, son of Teudor, now rules the two lands of Buallt and Gwytheyrnion. Teudor himself is king of the land of Buallt, son of Pascent, son of Guoidcant, son of Moriud, son of Eldat, son of Eldoc, son of Paul, son of Mepurit, son of Briacat, son of Pascent, son of Vortigern the Thin, son of Guitataul, son of Guitolin, son of Gloui.

50. Following his [Vortigern's] death, holy Germanus returned to his own land.

For Nennius' account of Germanus' purported connection with St Patrick (Chapter 51 of the *Historia*), see Chapter 5 of this work, under "Patrick".

The Corpus Christi College Cambridge manuscript of Nennius' *Historia* (MS CCCC 139), datable to September 1164, contains the following gloss dated c.1200:

> "This Vortimer son of Vortigern, in a synod held in Guartherniaun, after the unspeakable king on account of the incest which he had committed

with his daughter, had fled from the face of Germanus and from the clergy on Britannia, was unwilling to consent to the vileness of his father, but returning to St Germanus fell at his feet, asking pardon, and in atonement for the calumny put upon St Germanus by his father and sister, dedicated that land, whereon the aforesaid bishop had endured such opprobrium, to be his own for ever. Whence also in memory of St Germanus it took the name Guar[th]enniaun, which in Latin means *calumpnia iuste retorta*, calumny justly retorted, since, when he had thought to vituperate the bishop, it was himself he visited with vituperation."[10]

Notes

1) An echo of Ecclesiasticus 48:16?

2) Could Exodus 12:46 be the source of this story? It occurs in several forms in the "lives" of saints other than Germanus (Ciaran of Clonmacnoise, and Tathan of Gwent, for instance), and is not confined to the British Isles. See Greenhalgh and Eliopoulos, pp.101-102 for a version from Cappadocia, and Frazer, Chapter 53 for further treatment of this motif.

3) Nennius' account of heavenly fire, the need to remain behind closed doors to avoid seeing the destruction of Benlli's fort, and the eating of the calf bring to mind Genesis 19:17 and 24-26, Exodus 12:21-22 and Isaiah 26:20-21. Additionally, an

entry in the *Annales Cambriae* states that the fort of Deganwy (in Gwynedd) was burnt by lightning in the year 812: within Nennius' memory, if he composed the *Historia Brittonum* after that date. Similarly, heavenly fire destroys Baia's hall in Rhygyfarch's account (*c.*1091-1093) of the *Life of St David*.

A mighty Iron Age hillfort crowns the summit of Moel Fenlli ("Benlli's Mount") in the Clwydian Hills. The site of a homestead named Llys Fenlli ("Benlli's Court") stands about halfway up the slope. Early in the 19th century a hoard of about 1,500 Roman bronze coins was found on the hill, and in 1846 more Roman coins were found, including some gold and silver ones. Those which survive are generally of the period 330 – 350 AD, and those with legible mint marks were manufactured at Treves, Lyons and Arles in Gaul. Much Roman pottery (including a bowl of Argonne pottery, from the late fourth or early fifth century AD) and some glass has also been found, indicating, in all, that the fortress was occupied by a substantial native population during the period 100 – 400 AD.

A *cywydd* (ode) by Gruffydd ap Ieuan ap Llywelyn Fychan of Llannerch (c.1470 – 1520), attributes the death of Benlli the Giant to Cynhafal, patron saint of nearby Llangynhafal (*Cambrian Journal*, i (1854), p.217). According to John Jones of Gellilyfdy (c.1585 – 1657/8), there was a tradition that the Main Meirion ("Meirion's Stones") on Maes Mawr between Yale and Ystrad Alun marked the grave of Beli, son of Benlli the Giant, who was slain by Meirion ap Tybiawn. As the Black Book of Carmarthen says:

"Pieu y bed yn y maes mawr
balch y law ar y lafnawr:
bed beli ab benlli gawr.

"Whose is the grave on Maes Mawr?
He whose proud hand was upon his blade:
"The grave of Beli, son of Benlli the Giant."

The Chevalier Lloyd specifies that Maes Mawr is above Rhyd y Gyfarthfa, Llanferres.

Heiric gives a different version of the conflict between Germanus and Benlli, which omits the perspiring servant and his death, but states that Germanus succeeded in gaining an audience with the king, upbraided him, and pushed him from his throne with his episcopal staff, commanding him to make way for his betters. Whereupon Benlli and his family fled, and Germanus enthroned Cadell Ddyrnllwg ("Cadell Bright-hilt").

In his *Elegy for the Three Sons of Gruffydd ap Llywelyn*, Bleddyn Fardd sings of a battle between Benlli the Giant and Arthur:

"Gwaewddur ual arthur wrth gaer uenlli"
"Steely as Arthur by Benlli's Fort"

See also note 7 below.

4) 1 Samuel 2:8.

5) This description of placing a child on the lap of an important personage, and trimming the hair of its head, sounds like a rite of honourable formal adoption, here deliberately misconstrued to Vortigern's disadvantage. The importance of hair-trimming by a relative finds an echo in the tale of *Culhwch and Olwen*, and part of the Orthodox rite of Chrismation (usually following immediately after baptism) also involves the cutting of hair. The child is not named in this particular chapter, but bearing in mind his identification and fate as indicated in Chapter 48 of the *Historia*, one recalls that the cutting of hair is also part of the rite of entry into monasticism.

6) A tale very similar to that of the burying of Bendigeidfran's head at London, as recounted in the *Mabinogi*. Three churches consecrated in Germanus' name cluster around Lincoln (see Map 3).

7) See Chapter 6. Nennius also states that Vortigern's response to his defeat by the Saxons was to flee with his wizards (*magi*) to the "uttermost limits" of his kingdom, and attempt to build a fortress. He then recounts the tale of Ambrosius and the dragons, and how Vortigern gave that stronghold to Ambrosius: incidents connected with Dinas Emrys in Snowdonia. Chadwick (1954) offers the

possibility that this may originally have been a legendary contest between Germanus and the wizards, the saint being later displaced in the tale by Ambrosius "the fatherless child".

Then Vortigern went north (ad sinistralem plagam), to "Guunnessi" (or "Guenesi"), erecting there the fortress of "Cair Guorthigirn" (Vortigern's Fort). That's probably at the present Nant Gwrtheyrn ("Vortigern's Ravine") below the peaks of Yr Eifl on the Gwynedd coast, upon one of which stands the notable hillfort of Tre'r Ceiri. An ancient burial cairn, "Bedd Gwrtheyrn" (Vortigern's Grave) once stood there (see Chapter 6), and Gwynnys is nearby. One manuscript of the *Historia* states that Vortigern built the fortress of Guasmoric ("Old Carlisle", at present) between Carlisle and Cockermouth in Cumbria.

A stanza in the *Black Book of Carmarthen* records a tradition that Vortigern was buried at Ystyfachau:

E bet yn ystyuacheu
y mae paup yn y amheu.
Bet gurtheyrn gurtheneu.

*"The grave at Ystyfachau
Which everyone doubts [or: On which all look askance]:
The grave of Vortigern the Thin."*

Interestingly, this stanza follows immediately after another concerning the burial of Gyrthmul Wledig at Guynassed (comp. "Guunnessi\Guenesi" above), somewhere in the vicinity of Pont-lliw. The location of "Ystyfachau" is no longer known, though it has been speculated that the name could have changed to something like Stange (Llanddeusant, Carmarthenshire) or even Stanage (Knighton, Powys) by the time it came to be officially recorded centuries later.

8) In addition to his incineration by heavenly fire, Nennius also records that some said the earth opened and swallowed Vortigern, and others that he "lived in sorrow and disgrace". Humphrey Llwyd records a tale that the "King of Powys", his queen and all their family were engulfed in Pwll Llynclys (literally, "the court-swallowing pool") near Oswestry during Germanus' mission (see Chapter 8). The king's sin was to refuse Germanus a hearing, so the "king" in question could be Benlli, Vortigern, or some other ruler, now unknown.

9) "Renis" has been identified as Riez (Rhegium) in the south of France: though it must be pointed out that "he" in this passage could refer to St Germanus, who founded, according to the *Life of St Samson*, a monastery near the Severn. The name "Renis" is not entirely unlike "Hafren", the Welsh name of the Severn.

Nennius, however, in identifying the child as "Faustus", seems to imply that he was indeed that Faustus who became one of 5th-century Gaul's most prominent clerics. Born about 405-410, he was appointed abbot of Lérins (see Chapter 4) about the year 433, and Bishop of Riez in 462: he was present at a synod in Rome that year. Alcimus Avitus, Bishop of Vienne, and Sidonius Apollinaris call him a Briton, born in Britain or, perhaps, a Breton, born in Brittany. The similarity of Faustus' description of the ecclesiastical hierarchy to that found in the *Chronicon antiquissimum* composed in Britain before 578 may also hint at his origins.

A reference by Sidonius (*Euchariston ad Faustum Episcopum*) to Faustus' "hallowed mother" may refer to Faustus' earthly mother, or to the Church: though if the former, would hardly be suitable for one who conceived incestuously. Bishop Possessor of Africa calls Faustus a Gaul, perhaps because he had lived so long in that country. Gennadius says he was most erudite in the Scriptures (*Vir in divinis scripturis satis intentus*).

Sidonius Apollinaris was baptised by Faustus, and admired his philosphical and rhetorical abilities, saying that he had given public demonstration of his skill in forensic rhetoric (*in palaestris exerceris urbanis*). This could suggest, if he was indeed a Briton, that schools of rhetoric and philosophy still survived in 5th-century Britain (see Chapter 4; "Patrick" in Chapter 5, and K. Dark (2000)): but many of Faustus' circle were highly cultured men, adept at the art of public speaking.

If he was of royal stock, then possessing such

education and prestige as only royalty could afford, and even a blessing from Germanus himself (see below), would certainly have smoothed Faustus' path to high clerical office. Other comments by Sidonius suggest that Faustus maintained his contacts with Britain, including sending books of his works to Britain (or Brittany) through the offices of a venerable British hieromonk named Riocatus (see below). This suggests that Eastern intellectual and spiritual currents could flow far to the West, via Provence, despite the political disintegration of the Roman Empire. Nennius may have known of Faustus from such continental documentation.

Faustus was famed for his asceticism, preaching and attention to the welfare of the disadvantaged. An enemy of Arianism and Pelagianism, he came to the fore as leader of those supporting St John Cassian and Honoratus of Lérins' views on the relationship of Grace and works as means of salvation (see Chapter 4). He had a leading rôle in the peace negotiations with Euric the Visigoth in 474, but when the latter conquered Provence in 481, Faustus was exiled as an opponent of Arianism. He returned on Euric's demise, and lived until about 490-493.

10) Thus Wade-Evans 1941. As he comments, the passage is clearly connected with St Harmons in Gwrtheyrnion, Powys, playing on a pun deriving the territorial name "Gwrtheyrnion" ([Land of] Vortigern's People) from "gwarth" (disgrace), in

the form of a grant of land to the saint and, consequently, to his clerical successors. See also "St Harmons" in Chapter 6.

The Value of Nennius' Testimony

The oldest known manuscript of the *Historia* is Chartres MS 98, dating from about 900 AD. It is fragmentary, and especially interested in the activities of St Germanus. The most complete version is MS. Harleian 2859 (H), which also contains a series of British annals and Welsh geneaolgies, and was written *c.* 1100.

Nennius obviously drew on a native cycle of Germanus legends very different to the *Life* as given by Constantius of Lyons, and states that he obtained the account from "the *Book of Blessèd Germanus*". Heiric of Auxerre's work shows that this native British Germanus tradition was taken in some form or other to Burgundy about the end of the 9th century (see Chapter 2).

Perilous as it is to "argue from silence" (especially in the field of hagiography), the fact that Gildas, writing his *De Excidio Britanniae* about a century after Vortigern's time, does not mention Germanus; and that Constantius, writing but about fifty years after Germanus' earthly demise, does not mention Vortigern, suggests that the Germanus legends were initially unconnected with the story of Vortigern.

Nennius, knowing of differing traditions regarding the demise of Vortigern, chose the one which stressed the power of Germanus and the Church. He says nothing of

Pelagianism, nor of the Hallelujah Victory, or of other details of Constantius' account. He either knew nothing of that document, or judged its contents to be superfluous to his aims.

The Chatres text states that the chapters concerning Germanus were derived from "excerpts made by the son of Urbagen from the *Book of the Blessèd Germanus*". That Book is now lost, and we know nothing of it save what Nennius preserves. We may state that it was a very early work of Welsh hagiography, but should resist the temptation to conclude summarily that "the son of Urbagen" was Rhun ab Urien of Rheged, a prince of that north British realm *c.* 625 AD. Apart from the possibility that there was more than one "son of Urbgen" active between the 5th and 9th centuries, there appears also to have been a strong urge in Nennius' period to enlist the political prestige and cultural inheritance of Rheged both to support rival claims to political authority in Powys, and to bolster the authority of the rulers of nearby Gwynedd. The subject is interesting, but beyond the scope of this work. Suffice to say that these claims to dynastic legitimacy could have provided a millieu wherein a saga or legend of Germanus was conflated with those of Benlli, Vortigern and Rhun ab Urien, to political advantage. Those wishing to learn more of this subject may consult R. Bromwich and D. P. Kirby (see Bibliography).

If Nennius writes from the standpoint of a Gwynedd cleric, and as the kings of Gwrtheyrnion – if not all Powys – were descended from Vortigern, then his allegation of Vortigern's incest with his daughter may be but slinging mud at a ruling dynasty of a neighbouring kingdom, and the blackening of the memory of a king who was supposed to have tolerated Pelagianism (see Chapter 4). This, and Germanus' pursuit of Vortigern to Caer Gwrtheyrn in "the land of the men of Dyfed", echo Chapter 31 of Gildas' *De Excidio*: for there Gildas fulminates against Vortipor, King of Dyfed, and his "shameless" daughter. The same execratory urge may lie behind the claim that the House of Cadell (a Powys dynasty possibly opposed to that of Vortigern, and claiming descent from the rulers of Rheged) were descended from a mere servant. Nennius' imputation that the Bishop of Riez was incestuously conceived may also be an attack on Faustus' religious persuasion (see Chapter 4).

More concrete evidence regarding the importance of St Germanus' place in the history of Powys, as remembered in the ninth century, is provided by the inscription on Eliseg's Pillar (near Llangollen), which dates from about 800-825, i.e. about the time of the *Historia*'s composition. The following quotation from what remains of the inscription suggests the existence of strong local traditions concerning the founding of the kingdom:

"...Concenn....by his own hand...to his own kingdom, Powys...and...the mountain...the Kingship... Maximus... of Britain...Concenn, Pascent, Maun, Annan + Britu, additionally, [was] son of Guorthigirn, who was blessed by Germanus, and was born to him of Severa, daughter of King Maximus who slew the king of the Romans..."

(The inscription is now illegible, and we're indebted to

82

Edward Lhuyd's record for most of what we know of it.)

"Guorthigirn" means Vortigern: and far from execration, the inscription seems to trumpet a connection with that ruler, suggesting either that Germanus blessed a son of Vortigern's named Britu, or that Vortigern, Britu's father, was blessed by Germanus. No "Faustus" is mentioned.

Before dismissing Nennius' account as a complete fabrication, however, it remains possible that Britu was that Faustus of Riez whom Nennius suggests, however clumsily, to have been a fourth son of Vortigern's. Britu may have changed his name (as was the practice) when he became a monk. Jesus College MS XX, 14 records that Pascent son of Vortigern had a son named Riagath, i.e. the "Briacat" [? a mistake for "fab Riacat" (son of Riacat)] named by Nennius. If this guesswork is correct, then it's possible that Riagath son of Pascent was the monk "Riocatus" mentioned by Sidonius Apollinaris in 471 as "twice an exile", and that Faustus was his uncle. These days, one wouldn't expect a monk to have descendants: but there are instances in the past of high-born men becoming monks, and occasionally re-entering "the world" as political leaders. Constans son of Constantine III, and Maelgwn of Gwynedd, for instance.

The name "Britu" also occurs in the Harleian genealogies as a son of Cat(t)egirn or Cateyrn. Nennius (Chapters 44 and 48) has Cateyrn as a son of Vortigern: but in the genealogies, Cateyrn is a son of one Catell. Catell may be the Cadell Ddyrnllwg raised (according to Nennius) by Germanus to the throne of Powys, or an alternative form of Cateyrn.

In this thicket of possibilities, we should bear in mind that what few sources we have seldom agree regarding the number, names, descendants and order of Vortigern's offspring. There may have been many a "Britu" (Brutus), or the supposed name could itself be a mistake for "Vortigern of Britain". The possible existence of a widespread "Vortigern saga" once current in present-day Wales, Ireland, Scotland and Brittany, and the significance of the Breton *Life of St Gurthiern* as a parallel version of the Vortigern legend, is interestingly discussed by Chadwick (1954).

To sum: in the first quarter of the 9th century, there may have been two rival dynasties in Powys, i.e. those of Vortigern and of Cadell Ddyrnllwg. A ruler named Cyngen, of the House of Vortigern, thought it worth proclaiming that his ancestors had been blessed by St Germanus: a connection which may go a long way towards explaining the popularity of Germanus dedications on or near the territory of Powys. Nennius' work, however, may have tipped the balance against Vortigern and in favour of Cadell in the minds of later chroniclers and genealogists.

Geoffrey of Monmouth

Geoffrey of Monmouth wrote his immensely popular *Historia Regnum Britanniae* about the year 1136. It's very far from being a dependable record of events seven hundred years earlier, but contains two references to St Germanus. In Book VI, Chapter XIII, Sts Germanus and Lupus are mentioned as having visited Britain in order to quash heresy, and that "Gildas in his elegant essay has recorded their many miracles". In the following chapter, Vortimer son of Vortigern is said to have built many churches "at Germanus' instigation".

Geoffrey appears to have confused Nennius with Gildas, possibly because he was using a source such as the British Library Cotton Caligula AVIII manuscript of the *Historia Brittonum*, which names Gildas as its author.

4. Pelagianism

Any serious discussion of Pelagianism would require much more than can be afforded by this booklet: but as it is most relevant to any consideration of St Germanus, the writer dares touch upon the subject here in the hope that the better-informed may correct his mistakes.[1]

Inasmuch as it was expounded over time, and insofar as may be gleaned from disparate (and often hostile) sources, Pelagius' doctrine could be summarised as follows:

- Man is a special creature of God, in a special relationship with Him, and in His image. In consequence, he is endowed, by God's Grace, with fundamental rationality and an attunement to the divine will, expressed as conscience and natural goodness.
- God has planted in him the ability to discriminate between good and evil, and live without sin. He is aware that God wishes him to perform good, but is free to choose between good and evil. That man can be sinless shows that he was created by a just God.
- Man does not sin because of any necessity imposed on the will from without, and the needs of his own flesh do not lead inexorably to sin. Body and soul are not opposing substances, and the flesh does not force man to sin.
- Were it otherwise, and sin inevitably part of the human condition, man could not be held guilty. Rather, man sins by turning his will against his own nature, and against God's will.

- Original Sin is not transmitted through sexual reproduction, and no-one is guilty of sin who did not sin by his own will. Sin is not an essential component of human existence, and can neither damage, weaken nor change human nature.
- That which is in man at birth is that which God has created, and God creates no evil: therefore a child dying before baptism is not condemned. Children learn sin from those around them.
- Adam was the first sinner and through him sin came into the world. Despite this, a few men did live according to their essential nature and were sinless: Abel, Noah, Melchizedek, and Abraham, for instance.
- Most men, however, imitated Adam in disobeying God. They acted contrary to nature, and ignorance covered their reason like rust. The Law of Moses was a means of scraping clean and burnishing human reason, so that man could again know how to live without sin, and win eternal life. This Law is also Grace, and asks nothing of man that he could not achieve.
- God's Law, which alone can destroy habitual sin, may be seen in the Scriptures, which hold a mirror to man's condition. The Law of Moses succeeded in making mankind aware of sin: but most, gripped by vice and ignorance, persisted in their old ways. The Law of Moses needed to open out and develop into something stronger which would make us once more aware of our true nature, and how easily the paths of righteousness may be trod.
- Therefore Christ came into the world, as Redeemer (suffering that death on behalf of mankind by which sins are forgiven), Revealer of the way which leads to

eternal salvation, Example of sinlessness, and Bringer of that help which overcomes the power of sinful habits. This is Christ's Grace. It is not the Law alone, but the Law and Help.

- By His death, Christ has deleted the condemnation of mankind for the sins of the past; and by His forgiveness, teaching and example has broken the grip of sin, offering the real possibility of sinless life. God has thus reconciles us to Himself, and saves us, if we so desire: for He will not impose Grace upon us.
- Man cannot, by his own unaided nature, save himself. He can, however, live a sinless life, and obey Christ's commandments, without difficulty, for even before Christ's coming there were entirely sinless men. Therefore sin is neither inevitable nor excusable.
- Knowledge of the will of God comes before doing that will. Sinlessness cannot precede knowledge of the Law, as expressed in both Old and New Testaments. Doing is more important than knowing, but in point of time knowledge is prior.
- Faith originates in free choice, and is only the beginning. Full justification is not by faith alone, but by faith followed by works of righteousness.
- God's foreknowing predestination is both His will to make his Grace available to those whom He knows will come to Him in faith, and His will that future rewards be commensurate with moral achievement in this life.
- Baptism is the sacrament of justification by faith alone. In baptism one is absolved from past sins without respect to merit, and in that moment made "righteous". Righteousness is the condition of being guiltless of past sins: of believing in Christ, and

having fulfilled the whole of the Law. The formula "by faith alone" applies to that unique situation of the individual at his conversion and baptism: but after baptism, and pre-eminently at the Judgement, "righteousness" is dependent upon "works of righteousness", i.e. obedience to the moral precepts of Christ and the Apostles.

Man's nature, then, is essentially good, but dwelling in sinlessness requires great effort and iron discipline on the part of the believer. For as Adam was cast out of Eden in consequence of a single act, so one lapse on the part of the believer would be enough to condemn him or her entirely, as one who has sinned voluntarily.[2] Pelagians, therefore, tended to think themselves better, more upright than others: they were the "real Christians" (*integri Christiani*). The eventual aim was to form the perfect religious group: and to that end entirely Christian behaviour, the Christian Law, had to be forced upon all baptised members of the Church. The individual Pelagian could neither allow himself to sin nor tolerate sin in others.

Several commentators (e.g. St Augustine, Orosius, Prosper Tiro, Gennadius and Mercator) state that Pelagius was a Briton.[3] He describes himself as an "old man" in 404 AD, so he may have been born about the year 350. He had means enough to go to Rome about the year 382 in order to study law.[4] This was a period of great ferment and debate among western Christians, in particular, concerning the nature of Christian perfection: with Jovinian, Vigilantius, Origen, Manicheans, Augustine and others putting forth their views on this subject.

89

Appalled, perhaps, by a permissive attitude towards sin he encountered in Rome, Pelagius "quit the courts" in 386, "and betook himself to the Church" (*forum negligens se ad ecclesiam transtulit*), according to St Jerome:[5] but ever afterwards stressed the importance of the Law.

By 394 Jerome (and also Marius Mercator and others) calls Pelagius a "monk": which at that early date, may simply mean "an ascetic". He was never a priest, and Paulus Orosius and Pope Zosimus term him a "layman". He seems to have been mighty of body, a "huge, massive Goliath of a man, with his big, strong neck and his corpulence" according to Orosius, and a "tall, well-built man" (*grandis et corpulentus*), again according to Jerome.

Jerome also states that Pelagius was learned and able (*homo latinissimus et facundissimus*), and his theological works proved popular in Rome. He seems to have come under the influence of pagan philosophies such as Stoicism (which held that moral strength was enough to ensure the salvation of the soul); Rufinus of Aquileia, a translator of Origen and of the Enchiridion of Sixtus, and who held that Adam's sin had not been transmitted; Augustine's anti-Manichean works; and Julian of Eclanum, who favoured the institution of marriage and judged Jovinian, Mani and Augustine to err in denying the vital importance of free will during the entire course of the Christian life.

Pelagius may have met Jerome when the latter was in Rome during 382-385, and the discord between them may date from that time. They were certainly in dispute from 393 onwards, after the publication of Jerome's *Adversus*

Iovinianum, following which both accused each other of Origenism, and Pelagius accused Jerome of over-reacting to Jovinianism, thereby undermining the institution of marriage: an accusation not entirely devoid of substance.

Pelagius attracted a following amongst the upper classes, perhaps because the concept of an intellectual, religious élite (i.e. those more able to use their free will and reason in order to avoid sin) chimed with aspirations to social exclusivity. They also respected rigid self-discipline and the supremacy of reason as the moral inheritance bequeathed by their pagan ancestors, the *boni mores Romanorum*. Pelagianism, therefore, was most popular in Rome and other areas most under aristocratic influence, e.g. Campania and Sicily. He was in particularly good odour with widows and virgins in seclusion, and his remaining works reflect an abiding interest in the spiritual condition of women. No-one, however, accused him of impropriety: his moral character was impeccable. In these respects, he was similar to Jerome: perhaps uncomfortably so, for Jerome's peace of mind.

Pelagius would have been present in Rome during 400, when Pope Anastasius and the Emperor Honorius condemned Origenism. He may also have been aware of Rufinus' attack on Jerome in 401, accusing him of Origenism. Pelagius published his *Commentary on the Epistles of St Paul* in 410, setting forth the essentials of his doctrine: but faced with the Gothic invasion, fled Rome for Sicily, and was in Africa by Spring 411. That year, one of his associates, Caelestius, was twice arraigned before a synod at Carthage for his beliefs:[6] but by then Pelagius had already left Africa (shortly after June 411). He was in

Palestine by 414 at the latest, and there set about propogating his views, publishing his *De Natura* and *De libero arbitrio* in response to Jerome's teaching that sin is an inevitable consequence of man's corporeal existence.

Jerome, intensely worried and annoyed, feared that Pelagius was fanning the ashes of their old dispute, propogating Origenism, and making man out to be the equal of God. He counter-attacked with his *Letter to Ctesiphon*, *Dialogue against the Pelagians* (417), and *Commentary on Jeremiah*, tracing Pelagius' ideas back to Origen and Rufinius. Jerome tended, however, towards the "synergistic" view, i.e. co-operation between God and man, rather than thoroughgoing predestinationism: but that didn't prevent Pelagians from burning his monasteries in Jerusalem, forcing him to flee for his life to the security of a tower. In the meantime, news of this serious disturbance, and a copy of Pelagius' *De Natura*, reached the Bishop of Hippo in Numidia, Augustine.

Augustine hadn't met Pelagius whilst the latter was in Africa. He was preoccupied at that time with his struggle against the Donatists, and how one should react to the fall of Rome. He was not unacquainted with Pelagius and his works, and whilst in polite disagreement with him regarding some points of doctrine as expressed in the *Commentary on the Epistles of St Paul*, praised him respectfully as a "holy man" (*vir sanctus*) and prominent Christian.

During this period, however, Augustine was gradually developing his doctrine of Predestination; and in 413 preached, contrary to Caelestius, that infants are not sinless. This brought upon him accusations of innovation, even heresy, and the threat that the Eastern bishops would condemn him. The following year he wrote against some Sicilian Christians whose views seem to have owed much to Pelagius: but not against Pelagius himself, who had long decamped.

Reading Pelagius' *De Natura* in 415 disturbed him: but the real horror was that the author backed his views with a wealth of quotations from Catholic authors – Lactantius, Hilary of Poitiers, Ambrose, John Chrysostom, Xystus, Jerome and even Augustine himself. Pelagius, enlisting Catholic orthodoxy in his cause, was no longer a distant figure: he was a dangerous enemy who was laying claim to historical Christian theology, daring to imply that his views were those of the Fathers, *and of Augustine.* Augustine decided that Pelagius was intent on intruding into Christianity "the general spirit of pagan ethics, self-reliant, unappreciative of the absolute need of God" (Taylor). This denial of Original sin, in Augustine's view, rendered the Cross superfluous, and would destroy any belief among the faithful in that Grace bestowed to man through Jesus Christ.

Bishop John of Jerusalem, a friend of Pelagius', convened a synod in July 415 to investigate Pelagius' orthodoxy. Augustine sent his pupil, Orosius, to oppose Pelagius: but Orosius was intemperate, and hampered by his lack of Greek, whereas Pelagius stood his ground. The synod refrained from passing judgement, refering the subject back to the Western ecclesiastical authorities, as Pelagius, Jerome and Origen were all Latins.

93

Orosius blamed his interpreter.

Then two Gaulish bishops, Heros of Arles and Lazarus of Aix-en-Provence, arrived in Palestine, and at their request a second synod concerning Pelagianism was held at Diospolis (Lydda) in December 415. With Eulogius, Metropolitan of Caesarea presiding, thirteen other bishops in attendance, and both Heros and Lazarus unable or unwilling to be present, Pelagius explained that there can be no salvation without God's Grace, as all men are created by Him. He also said that much of Caelestius's work did not reflect his (Pelagius') opinion: and in evidence of his own Orthodoxy, produced a letter from Augustine, written in 412. It was decided that Pelagius was Orthodox, and in full communion with the Church.

With Pelagianism gaining ground, Augustine went on the attack, publishing *De Natura et Gratia* and other anti-Pelagian works. At Aurelius' direction, the bishops of the province of Africa held a synod in autumn 416, during which Pelagius' and Caelestius' teachings were condemned, and they themselves declared heretics. Shortly afterwards, Augustine convened a similar synod in Numidia, with the same result. Augustine and four bishops then contacted Pope Innocent, sending him a copy of *De Natura* with the offending passages underlined. In January 417 Innocent gave his seal of approval to the African and Numidian bishops' decisions, severing the Pelagians' communion with the Church.

Pelagius wrote to Pope Innocent in conciliatory terms, stressing his orthodoxy, and condemning Manichees,

Montanists, and "those who hold, with Jovinian, that man cannot sin": but Innocent died before the letter reached him. Despite Innocent's support, Augustine and the African bishops' denouncement of Pelagianism as a heresy didn't go down well with the succeeding pope, Zosimus. Having received the letter intended for Innocent, and spoken personally with Caelestius, he judged the action taken against Pelagius to be a usurpation of Rome's prerogative to decide upon such matters, and that only after hearing evidence from both sides. In the meantime, he "bore emphatic testimony to the orthodoxy of Pelagius and Caelestius, and described their chief opponents, Heros and Lazarus, as worthless characters, whom he had visited with excommunication and deposition. They, in Rome, he says, could hardly refrain from tears, that such men [as Pelagius and Caelestius], who were so often mentioned in *gratia Dei* and the *adjutorium divinum*, should have been condemned as heretics" (Schaff, Vol. 3, 9.149).

It was recalled that the bishops of Africa had made false accusations in the past. Caelestius's visit to Rome in 417 may also indicate that he too was willing to be reconciled, but the Augustinian party refused to yield an inch or present further testimony: and who knows what may have happened, had the government not stepped into the fray by publishing the indictment against the Pelagians despite Zosimus' doubts. This was a most unusual step, provoked, no doubt, by fears of the social and political consequences of radical Pelagianism: but Zosimus soon followed the Emperor's lead, finally confirming Pelagianism to be a heresy in 418.[7]

That year, at the request of the three Christians Albina, Pinianus and Melania, who were anxious to heal the rift between the opposing parties, Pelagius condemned anyone who "thinks or says that God's Grace is not necessary for every hour, moment and act of our lives". That is the last we know of him.[8] The same three also wrote to Augustine, stressing Pelagius' Orthodoxy (as they perceived it): but Augustine's response was to publish his *De Gratia Christi*.

We last hear of Caelestius in Constantinople in 429, and the Emperor Theodosius II expelled the Pelagians from there in 430. The following year Pelagianism was condemned by the Ecumenical Council of Ephesus, under Cyril of Alexandria. The Council seems to have rubber-stamped the Pope of Rome's decrees regarding the subject, and Cyril's interest in it was principally motivated by a desire to alert the Papacy to the threat of Nestorianism: but the conciliar decision finally brought to an end any support that doctrine may have had in the East.

Augustine knew, however, that Pelagianism would not be defeated in the absence of a convincing counter-doctrine. So his undoubted talents brought forth the doctrine of Predestination, and the crowning of Grace as the sole means of salvation. In short:

- When Adam fell, all mankind fell with him. We are all participants in that Fall, and all guilty of it. Sin is so deeply rooted in our nature that not even conversion and baptism can divorce us from our past, and the consequences of our disobedience.

- Mankind is so depraved and powerless that we cannot avoid sin: we have no freedom of choice or action. Therefore:
- all are completely dependent upon the free gift of divine mercy.
- As that mercy is wholly uncompelled, it need not save anyone: not mankind as a whole, nor any specific individual. God, by His Grace, will save according to His divine will, and the saved have been chosen by him since before the world was made. Therefore:
- the saved and lost have been predestined before birth, and no works on our part will change that in the least.
- Grace is irresistible and indefectible.
- Predestination is absolute, irrespective of forseen character.

Rather than aim for the Pelagian "perfect life", Augustinism foresees that we, in our frailty, will sin, and perhaps repent: but never, as long as we live, lose a tendency to sin again. Life will be one long temptation, but if God wills it, even a sinner lacking in good works can be gradually saved by faith and prayer. One way of expressing the difference between Augustinism and other doctrines may be that the former holds that original sin alone precedes salvation or condemnation, but others (including Pelagianism) hold that original sin and active sin determine our ultimate fate.[9]

In removing the need for any radical divide between the sinful past and the virtuous present, it may be said that Augustine's views represent a "Christianity of

97

Continuation". A Christian can continue to live in society as it stands, neither destroying nor radically refashioning it. It's no surprise that the authorities in Rome looked favourably upon this doctrine.[10]

The dispute between the Augustine's and Pelagius' followers exploded even unto bloodshed, with that extreme bitterness typical of a family feud. The Pelagians accused Augustine of being a pagan fatalist, a Manichee (as he himself admitted he was formerly),[11] and of disregarding the sacrament of baptism. The Augustinians accused the Pelagians of attempting to usurp God's omniscience with fallible human reason, and of denying the necessity of Grace.[12]

Parts of the Empire were untouched by the clash, or at least succeeded in keeping it at arm's length for the time being. In the East, for instance, the relationship between Grace and Works was not a subject of debate: and in Gaul, in one area where the influence of the East was strong (thanks to the presence of St John Cassian, amongst others), and the Emperor's domination on the wane, Church leaders held a doctrine regarding Grace and Works which avoided the extremes of either disputant party. Their centre was the monastery of St Honoratus on the isles of Lérins.[13]

Having opposed Leoporius of Trêves' form of Pelagiansm prior to 425,[14] they were then faced with Augustinism when copies of Augustine's *Libri contra Julianum* and *De Correptione et Gratia* reached Provence, the latter in 427. John Cassian responded with his *Thirteenth Conference*. On the foundations of the Scriptures and other elements of

98

the Tradition, the "Massilians" (as Chadwick terms them) disagreed with both Pelagianism and Augustinism.[15] I venture to sum up their doctrine as follows:

- Salvation lies within reach of all men.
- No man's attempts to win salvation, however eager, are sufficient unless safeguarded by Divine Love.
- Even before the Fall, free will could not attain unto salvation without God's Grace.
- Man's nature in general was corrupted by the Fall: but God's Love can overcome that, and He would that all be saved.
- God foreknows, and judges accordingly: but does not predestine.
- The Fall disabled human volition to a great extent, but neither destroyed it completely nor deprived it entirely of Grace. There remains in us an unquenchable spark kindled by God. If we safeguard that spark, it can co-operate with God unto our salvation.
- Grace is not always dependent on human merit, nor always precedent.
- Grace is essential, but conditional upon the free self-determination of the human will.
- Salvation depends upon co-operation between God and man. Perfection may be attained if man desires it, and struggles for it: but he cannot succeed in the absence of God's Grace.
- Sovereign Grace is God's: complete responsibility is man's.
- As men we have free will, which tends towards sin: but we are directed and compelled to better ends by God, even against our will at times.

In the opinion of the "Massilians", Pelagianism put too much stress on man's abilities, and Augustinism went to the other extreme, disempowering man completely and depriving him of free will and moral responsibility. This rendered religious effort useless, and encouraged negligence or despair. Pelagianism, they judged, was an innovation which one erring person had tried to introduce into the Church's outlook without his fully realizing the consequences. Augustine, in trying to withstand that, had himself come up with his own innovative and highly speculative ideas, rather than look to the true doctrine of the Church.[16]

They did not perceive their viewpoint as a kind of "no man's land" between two opposing positions. Rather, it was an attempt to stand by the apostolic tradition ("that which has been believed always, everywhere and by all", as St Vincent of Lérins puts it) in the face of two recent, unfounded and misleading doctrines. As Owen Chadwick points out, these men were "no mere clique of heresy, but a body containing leading bishops, priests and monks of Provence, united in the righteous conviction that they were representing the true Christian tradition." Their response showed the strength of their grip upon learning, tradition and theology; the deep spiritual inheritance of the East; and a practical attitude towards living the Christian life by combining correct belief with correct action (James 2:14-17). This practicality led many of them to combine monastic discipline with the work of shepherding the Christians of Gaul, urban and rural, at such an appallingly violent and unsettled time.[17]

St Germanus' links with the "Massilians" are too close to allow speculation that he was not aware of their views, or was not of the same persuasion. He was a friend of Hilary of Arles and a fellow-labourer of Lupus, two disciples of Honoratus of Lérins whose works show that they were of the same opinion concerning Pelagianism and Augustinism. Germanus' second visit to Britain was in the company of Severus, one of Lupus' disciples. In order to maintain such personal links, and co-operate with such men, Germanus must have been of the very same theological stuff.[18] One cannot safely suggest that he came to Britain in order to promote Augustinism, unless one allows for a radical change in his theological views between the first and second visits. A possibility, but one unevidenced.

The controversy continued long after Augustine's death in 430. As late as 452AD, the *Gaulish Chronicle* noted the year 418 as "the year Augustine is said to have devised the heresy of Predestination".[19] St John Cassian and the Massilians' doctrine was condemned by Augustine's followers at the Second Synod of Orange and the Synod of Valence in 529, and this decision was ratified by Pope Boniface II in 531. It was first (insultingly) termed "Semi-Pelagianism" in 1577: "Anti-Augustinism" would be nearer the mark. [20]

Pelagianism in Britain

British clerics sometimes travelled far in order to participate in Church councils, with bishops attending the Councils of Sardica (343), Sofia (347) and Rimini (359). St Paula of Bethlehem, writing to Rome at the beginning of the fifth century, states that "Even the Briton, remote from our world...seeks the spot he knows by fame and from the Scriptures": so there were means enough for new theological ideas to reach Britain in a comparatively short time. A form of Pelagianism was being preached in Gaul by Leoporius of Trêves prior to 425: and Prosper (Tiro) of Aquitane, a dependable chronicler and strong supporter of Augustinism, states that Pelagianism was brought to Britain by 429 by Agricola, son of the Pelagian Bishop Severianus. This would suggest that the doctrine was not here present before that date. Severianus may have been a Gaulish bishop, or an Italian one, as Pelagianism had its supporters there, also: but it is not stated that Agricola was a cleric. If present in Gaul, some Pelagians could have fled to Britain in the face of the barbarian invasions or the Armorican rebellion and its aftermath.

Prosper's words in praising the acts of the anti-Pelagian Pope Caelestinus I (422-432) ("...he rid Britain of that same disease, when he expelled from even that hidden recess on the ocean some enemies of Grace who had taken possession of the land of their birth...") could suggest that Britons were responsible for bringing Pelagianism from the Continent to their native land: or that Britons, rather than foreigners, led Pelagianism in Britain. Myres (1960) suggests that the self-assertiveness of Pelagianism may have held some appeal to those political leaders in Britain who, by their own militant efforts, had revolted against Rome and overcome barbarians: but there's no evidence to support a symbiosis of Pelagianism and British Nationalism *contra* Catholicism and Roman Imperialism (see Chapter 1, Note 10).

102

Morris (1965) argues that the Pelagian essay *de Vita Christiana* seems to have been written with an eye on conditions current in Britain during the 407-410 revolt, and that the author was shocked to learn that some people in other countries embrace the dogma of original sin. The essay is directed at a widow named Fatalis, and it's known that Pelagius wrote a letter to someone of the same name. Gennadius (*de Viris Inlustribus*, 57) says that the British Bishop Fastidius wrote on this theme: but perhaps Gennadius errs in this, and that Fastidius' text is not *de Vita Christiana*, but the one now known as *Admoneo te*.

It has been argued that the first letter (*Honorificantiae tuae*) in Caspari's collection, if not all six of them, was written in Sicily by a Briton very supportive of radical Pelagianism: but there's room to believe that the author may equally well have come from Rome or Spain.

It's possible that Caelestius the Pelagian was of Irish descent, perhaps from one of the Irish communities then flourishing in the western part of the Island of Britain. Gildas, writing about a century later, is under the impression that another piece of Pelagian literature, *de Virginitate*, was composed by a Briton (Fastidius again, perhaps).

It has been proposed that as Britain was free of the Emperor's grasp by 418, it's unlikely that Honorius' interdict would have had any force here. By the time Valentinian the III's interdict was published in 425, southern Gaul was under Visigothic rule, and the Emperor's writ no longer ran there, either. It appears, therefore, that the pillars of the Church in Britain and Gaul did not respond to Pelagianism in the same manner as those in Rome, or as suddenly. However, Constantius' remark about the exiling of Pelagians following Germanus' second visit to Britain suggests that Honorius' interdict was operative by 437 (or 447/8) in that part of Britain which Germanus visited. A result, perhaps, of the success of his previous visit of 429 in order to re-establish public support for Catholicism. It would be a mistake to think that the Britons had finally severed all ties with Rome in 410, and it's likely that they still considered themselves Roman citizens decades afterwards. Prosper Tiro refers to Britain up to 432 AD as a "Roman island"[21], and Gildas says that the Britons appealed for Aëtius' help sometime about 446 – 454. This piece of information from Constantius may witness that the Roman government's influence persisted for many years after Honorius advised the Britons to "look to their own defence".

Yet at first glance it doesn't seem that the debate concerning Pelagianism excited much response in Britain itself. That is to say, the Church, on the whole, seems to have remained in a "pre-Pelagian" condition, which could allow a spectrum of opinions regarding the relationship between Grace and Reason, if the subject was discussed at all. Constantius makes no mention of Germanus' having met any bishop or civil leader other than the military tribune and Elafius who, although highly placed, came to seek the healing of their children, not to hear a debate. One gets the impression that the clash between Germanus and the Pelagians may have been a local matter concerning two parties peripheral to the life of the Church in Britain as it then was. It's difficult to believe that church leaders would have been unaware of so momentous a happening as the visit of a Gaulish bishop, or that it could have happened without the approval of the civil authorities (Vortigern and his supporters). They seem to have tolerated the presence of Pelagians, but to have judged it best not to get involved in any dispute.

From the standpoint of Rome and the Continent, understanding that the Church in Britain still tolerated "Pelagian" attitudes could have given the impression that Pelagianism had "revived" there, and that direct advice and action was needed. A precedent for Germanus' visit may be found in the visit to Britain of Victricius, Metropolitan of Rouen about the year 396, in order to sort out a serious and complex dispute – though one unclear to us today – amongst the members of the Church.[22] It has been moved that his visit was somehow connected with Pelagianism: but it seems to have dragged on until 403, when Victricius received a letter (the *Liber Regularum*) from Pope Innocent I regarding ecclesiastical practice and discipline.

That, however, isn't the only possible interpretation. It's argued that Pelagianism couldn't have been in dispute in 396, as it wasn't outlawed until 418. The difficulty may rather have been that the Church in Britain was too divided and insufficiently confident in 396 to decide upon some subject or other (the procedure for ordinating bishops and archbishops, perhaps,) without asking outside aid. So in 429 also: the British bishops had failed to tackle Pelagianism themselves (perhaps because they lacked sufficient theological understanding), so once again they looked abroad for help.

Had Pelagianism reared its head in 396, it's unlikely that British bishops would have waited until 429 before seeking outside aid, without any Continental chronicler mentioning anything about it in the meantime. Had not Hilary of Poitiers praised the bishops of Britain for their stand against Arianism (*De Synodis*, 358-9)? And Athanasius the Great likewise in about 350 (*Apologia contra Arianos*)? Had not St John Chrysostom (402) and St Jerome lauded their constancy towards Catholicism? Whatever their faults, they were staunchly conservative and no friends of heresy: so when Pelagianism arrived in Britain in 429, they knew it for what it was, but had not the means to defeat it themselves. So they quickly and naturally appealed for help to the bishops of the nearest Roman province. Constantius may have refrained from mentioning this lest he reveal their weakness and impotence.

Prosper of Aquitaine, writing his *Epitoma Chronicon* scarcely four years after the event, states that Pope Caelestinus I, Zosimus' successor, sent Germanus to Britain as his own representative (*vice sua*) at the request of the deacon Palladius, and makes no mention of any Gaulish synod. Which is to say that Germanus was a papal legate with authority to act as he saw fit: an unusual appointment, which would only be allowed in an emergency where quick and decisive action was needed. The appointment of Palladius as bishop "to the Irish believing in Christ" in 431 may be viewed as an attempt to extinguish Pelagianism in those Irish communities in the west of Britain, if not in Ireland itself.[23] As Prosper says (*Contra Collatorem*, 21), the Pope, "in consecrating a bishop for the Irish, whilst striving to make the Roman island Catholic, also made the barbarian island Christian". Writing two or three years after this event, however, his tone implies that Palladius' mission had ended, and was probably unsuccessful. Prosper may have obtained information regarding Palladius and Germanus during visits to Rome in 430 and 431.[24]

Germanus' second visit had the same aim: Rome was determined to destroy heresy in Britain. Though Britain was not then ruled by the Emperor, the intention may have been to reverse that situation as soon as the barbarians were defeated on the Continent. Independent or not, it was feared that Britain was close enough to allow the Pelagians to regroup before reintroducing their doctrine to the Empire.

Despite these efforts on the part of Rome, it seems that parts of the West, including Britain and Ireland, long remained in that condition wherein Pelagianism could be tolerated, if unconsciously. The Pelagian *Liber Praedestinatus* seems to have been written in Rome, of all places, about the year 440. Gildas, in composing his *De Excidio Britanniae* somewhere in western Britain during the period 545-49, seems to have known nothing of either Pelagianism or Germanus, for otherwise he'd have been sure to give prominence to such important happenings.[25] Furthermore, he quotes from a Pelagian work which he had at hand (e.g. his stress that sacramental authenticity is promised *omni sancti sacerdoti* alone, in *de Excidio*, 109), without any indication that such a thing was unorthodox. This could indicate that the struggle between Pelagianism and Catholicism never touched Gildas' part of Britain, or that the argument was long forgotten by time he set pen to parchment. If Rhygyfarch's account of the Life of St David is accurate, then Pelagianism was still to be found in 6th-century Wales (see Chapter 5).

Pope John IV (640-642) saw fit to remind the Church in Ireland in 640 that Pelagianism was a heresy (see Bede, *Historia*, Book 2, Chapter 19): but Pelagius' *Commentary on the Epistles of St Paul*, under his name, was in use in Wales, Ireland and England until at least the beginning of the 8th century, almost three hundred years after the original Papal condemnation of Pelagianism. There are early Irish references to Pelagius in the *Collectio Canonum Hibernensis*, and in the Book of Armagh's *Prologues to the Pauline Epistles*, dating from about the last quarter of the 8th century.[26] Bede, who loathed Pelagianism, never accuses his Irish contemporaries of heresy.

Pelagianism must have struck a chord amongst the Empire's inhabitants, for about seventy Pelagian works remain, though often camouflaged under the names of wholly Unpelagian authors such as Augustine, Jerome and some popes. Camouflage or not, they were popular, and it seems that most of them were copied in northern European monasteries: an area where monastic missionaries from Britain and Ireland were notably active.[27]

This is not to say that Pelagianism ever truly struck root here. There's no sign that anyone in Britain, Ireland or the Continent subsequently regarded the inhabitants of these islands as any other than full members of the Catholic

108

Church, indicating that the Church in Britain, whatever the state of her earthly leadership, had defused any real challenge posed by Pelagianism. It would be pleasing to consider this the result of Germanus' visits, and that his mission to reinforce the Church in Britain, better her theological understanding and strengthen her contacts with the remainder of the Church, was very successful.[28]

Notes

1) The present writer here relies heavily upon R. F. Evans' *Pelagius: Inquiries and Appraisals* (see Bibliography).

2) Perhaps Pelagianism, in this respect, drew on a very ancient Christian belief that the believer is allowed only one opportunity to repent, and that immediately before baptism, probably (see Chapter 1, note 14). To sin afterwards would be to invite perdition. It may be based on Hebrews 6:4-6 and 10:26, and 1 John 5:18: and is prominent in the first parts of the *Shepherd* of Hermas (e.g. Vision 2, Chapter 2 and Mandate 4, Chapter 1), written about 135-150 AD. Writing about 397 AD, however, Sulpicius Severus has a demon voice this belief in Chapter 22 of his *Life of St Martin*.

The *Shepherd* of Hermas also declares infants to be entirely sinless, "for all babes are glorious before God, and are in the first place before Him" (Parable 9, Chapter 29). Testimony that this work was known to St John Cassian can be found in his *Second Conference of Abbot Severus*, Chapter XVII.

3) There seems little room to doubt that St Jerome (*Praef. in Jerem.*, Books I and III) in calling one of the Pelagian leaders an Irishman (*habet enim progeniem Scoticae gentis de Britannorum vicina*), stuffed with Irish porridge (*Scotorum pultibus proegravatus*), refers to Pelagius himself. Was he mistaken, or did Pelagius indeed hail from Ireland, or one of the Irish communities in Britain? The only other eminent associate of Pelagius' who could fit the bill (by default) is Caelestius, of whose origins nothing is now known. Thomas Pennant, writing in 1778, states that Pelagius was a product of the monastery of Bangor Is-coed in north Wales, but quotes no authority for his claim.

4) It isn't inconcievable that he arrived in continental Europe in the train of Magnus Maximus in 383 AD. Magnus established his court at Treves, and was in good odour with St. Martin of Tours, St. Ambrose of Milan, and Pope Siricius of Rome.

5) This suggests that Pelagius had been trained as an orator before taking up the legal profession. If so, it's evidence, firstly, that the Roman art of rhetoric was handed down in Britain until the mid 4th century, if not later (see D. Howlett): and secondly, that a Briton of those times could amass enough wealth to travel to Rome and embark on a career there. Note that references in the statutes of that time to *gratia* ("grace") are usually negative, meaning "corruption", "bribery", "irresponsible behaviour", and so forth.

6) Aurelius, Bishop of Carthage, refused to ordain Caelestius deacon, so the latter went to Ephesus, where he was ordained priest. It's possible that Canon 109 of the Council of Carthage (419) is aimed at a belief held by Caelestius or others in Carthage :

"Whosoever says that Adam, the first man, was created mortal, so that whether he had sinned or not, he would have died in body…not because his sin merited this, but by natural necessity – let him be anathema."

but it's highly unlikely that Pelagius believed so. "Mortal" in this context has shades of meaning, inasmuch as any created entity could be termed "mortal", or at least open to spiritual death. For a fuller discussion of this point, see Hieromonk Damascene, 2008.

7) The formation of groups and parties in late 4th-century Rome may be viewed as symptomatic of the disintegration of a society both divided and uncertain in the face of military and economic decline. With the coming of the Goths in 408, however, and their sack of Rome in 410, the Romans had to unite or die: no divisiveness could be tolerated. Between 410 and 418, therefore, there was a strong tendency towards recentralization.

Faced with riots both for and against Pelagianism in Rome in 417 and 418, the Emperor Honorius decided, on the 30th of April 418, to outlaw

111

Pelagianism. Pelagians, he stated, "think that to be of the same opinion as everyone else is a sure mark of low birth and insignificance: and that the hallmark of exceptional wisdom is to undermine that which is unanimously agreed". He ordered their arrest, their arraignment before a public tribunal and, if judged guilty, their eternal exile. Those who did not suffer this fate were scattered, and some may have made their way to Britain, where the Emperor's will no longer held force. The interdict was renewed in 425.

The dispute regarding Pelagianism may have been largely confined to ecclesiastical and intellectual circles, but the authorities viewed any doctrine which fostered ideological division, or closed the chasm between rich and poor, as an incitement to social rebellion at a time of extreme instability. It was feared that the Pelagians' tendency to attack *gratia*, "corruption" and "antisocial behaviour", and their opposition towards both wealth and the wealthy, would strike a chord amongst those ground into serfdom by the oppressive, authoritarian, pitiless and failing machinery of the Empire in the West.

The Pelagian belief that man could cast off sin did lead some extreme Pelagians to argue that society as a whole could also rid itself of such sinful behaviour as the amassing of wealth at the expense of the poor: "down with the rich" (*tolle divitem*) was one of their slogans. Julian of Eclanum idealized the life of the simple countryman as that of Adam before the Fall: a condition to which one could, and should, return. Simplicity was the key to the blessèd life, and the Pelagian attitude towards bodily needs favoured the sharing of earthly goods (especially with the poor), whilst frowning upon all material superfluity and excess. In this Pelagians could be compared to the Levellers or Diggers of 17th-century England, representing a tendency, which arises in Christianity every so often, to sweep away society's sinful past, and begin anew (a "Christianity of Discontinuation").

But as already implied, Pelagian radicalism did not include toleration. As Brown says:

"The Pelagians, to a depressing extent, were Late Roman men. To them, as to everyone else in that absolutist age, reform meant only one thing: reform from the top downwards; even more laws, sanctioned by even more horrifying punishments...Being a reformer in the Late Roman Empire meant being an absolutist – and the Pelagians were no exception."

So despite claims that their attitude to human nature was "optimistic", and that mankind was, in their view, "morally healthy", they were not liberals by a long chalk. Indeed, the spread of their doctrine has been compared to a "flood of chilling puritanism".

8) Bearing in mind that at least one Pope, two

113

ecclesiastical synods, at least thirty-two bishops and several prominent contemporary Christians had failed to find fault with Pelagius' teachnigs, and that almost all of what we know about them comes from the works of his bitter enemies, the possibility must be admitted that his own views, especially towards the end of his life, were not as extreme as some claimed. His ideas may also have been used as a platform by those of far mor radical tendencies.

9) Despite their differences, both Pelagianism and Augustinism both tend to lead to the same conclusion. In order to accept a doctrine and cling to it, there must be sufficient proof that fidelity will have the expected results, in part if not in whole: fruits which can be enjoyed now, in this world, as a foretaste of complete doctrinal fulfilment in the world to come. The distinguishing feature of Pelagianism, in this world, is that "True Christians" lead a disciplined and spotless life: they sin not. So also Predestination: irreproachable behaviour, and material success (following moral integrity) mark the "saved" out to the degree that they're obviously distinguishable from others. There arises an increasing stress on morality and external characteristics: on being visibly foremost in piety and commendable behaviour. Whilst not harmful in themselves, the increasing weight of such accretions may suffocate the "inner life", and the true state of the heart is neglected.

Practically, this opens a social gulf between the "saved" and the remainder: the "Lifestyle 'A'" and "Lifestyle 'B'" typical of Welsh communities under the strong influence of Calvinism, for instance. In such circumstances, the "saved" tend to isolate themselves: by endogamy, for instance. They may influence their community strongly if they gain economic and political power, and be successful in maintaining dominance for as long as they can maintain rigorous social stability: but as external influences seep in, it becomes increasingly difficult for them to assert authority. In that case, far from "saving" all about them, they become increasingly irrelevant, and wither.

Calvinism isn't the only faith to experience this movement from the internal to the external. Drifting, with time, further and further away from the light and warmth of the coming of the Spirit amongst us, we tend to give increasing importance to keeping rules and performing rites, and on morality and behaviour. The weaker our religion, the stronger our interest in morality, as Macaulay wrote. Orthodoxy itself trod this path, as in the case of the Russian Old Believers, and the general tendency of the Russian Orthodox Church of the 18th century to stress the letter of the law, and salvation by means of ascetic feats. Despite which, the Spirit continued to kindle the hearts of such saints as Paisius Velichovsky and Seraphim of Sarov.

10) It has been suggested that Pelagianism is an

"optimistic" response to the fall of Rome in 410, and Augustinism a "pessimistic" one: but the kernel of the argument predates that event.

As a good number of Roman aristocrats were but nominally or uncertainly Christian, it could be argued (despite that stated above regarding Pelaginaism's appeal to the *boni mores Romanorum*) that Augustinism, with it's comparative tolerance towards human weakness, would be more likely to draw the élite into the Church's fold, once and for all, than would strict, no-second-chances Pelagianism. In supporting Augustine, the Empire's spiritual and political leaders may have been aware of that. It should also be borne in mind that this dispute was taking place at the time of the Christianization of the Roman Senate, the aristocracy's very den. More accurately, the power of the Senate in Rome itself was dissolving, and recrystallizing in that city about the Church, a body unified under the leadership of the Pope. Such nobles as remained in Rome could either languish in a venerable but increasingly impotent Senate, or go with the flow, cleave to the prevailing doctrine of Catholicism (as opposed to Pelagianism), and find positions of influence in the Church. The arguments and politicking regarding who would be Pope (and ultimate dispensor of power) would persist down the centuries, but after 418 the leadership was never challenged on the basis of doctrine.

The other side of this coin was that the Church

inherited something of senatorial or even imperial power and influence. We see in the *Life of St Germanus* and other records how priests and bishops had to fill lay rôles formerly the preserve of generals or tribunes. We also see local chieftains, even invading "barbarians", allowing representatives and missionaries of the Church to establish themselves on old Roman military sites, as if it were wholly natural and expected that priests and monks, a new "Roman army", should inherit premises abandoned by the legions, such as Holyhead on Anglesey, or Burgh Castle in East Anglia, for instance. Such sites may also have been chosen because they were already enclosed, thus fulfilling the monastic need for a divide between "sacred" and "profane" space. Where such walls were lacking, an embankment or fence would need to be erected (as at Bangor, Gwynedd).

11) Manicheanism distinguishes between the "elect" and the "learners".

12) Pelagianism also comes unstuck on the matter of infant baptism. According to that doctrine, if sins are forgiven in baptism, this must happen with the consent and will of the believer. Yet is it to be administered to infants with the same formula as applies to adults, "in the remission of sins", even though infants are supposedly sinless by virtue of their inability to employ rational will.

13) The present writer believes it significant that Heros and Lazarus, Pelagius' opponents, were

bishops in this very area (see notes 6 and 7 above). Monasticism spread from Egypt to Italy and Gaul following St Athanasius, Patriarch of Alexandria's periods of exile in Trier and Rome, and his subsequent publication of a *Life of St Anthony*. The *Life of Paul the Hermit* by St Jerome, and works such as St Pachomius' (e.g. the *Lausiac History*) and St John Cassian's *Institutes* and *Conferences* were further stimuli. A great many monks and hermits were attracted to the isles and promontories of the Tyrrhenian Sea, such as Lipari, Gorgona and Sardinia. St Ambrose and St Jerome mention them, and the poet Rutilius Namatianus, voyaging from Rome to Aquitaine in 417, speaks contemptuously in his *De Reditu Suo* of islands full of "deluded" men "in dirty clothes, who call themselves by a Greek word, 'monachos'": a disgust shared by many, both pagans and Christians, at that time.

St Hilary of Poitiers (c.315-367) recorded the presence of groups of ascetics in his own city, and a number of hermits came together in a *monasterium* at Marmoutier under the leadership of St Martin of Tours: inspired, perhaps, by Hilary's experience of such communities in Cappadocia. However, the first monastery (in the sense of an organized cœnobic community) on the Gaulish mainland, the Abbey of St Victor by Marseilles, was founded by St John Cassian (c.360 - ?by 458). Whether a native of Gaul or of present-day Romania, he spent years under the guidance of leading monastics in Syria and Egypt. He wrote copiously of the monastic life, stressing the love of

God and practical purity of heart, rather than the theoretical. The stamp of Eastern attitudes and practice was evident on the institutions of Provence, and under his influence there arose many leading clerics famous for their learning, their denial of worldly comforts, and their great love towards the poor.

Following his journey to Greece, St Honoratus (c.350 – c.429) founded a monastery, a veritable nursery of holiness, on the smaller of the Isles of Lérins (present-day St-Honorat) near Cannes. Eucherius (in *De Laude eremi*) says that the saints of Lérins brought eastern hermits thence, and with them the practice of building separate cells for each monk. Both the eremitic and the conventual lives were led there. The monastery supplied the Church in Gaul with four metropolitans and at least thirteen bishops, including Hilarius of Arles (Honoratus' successor as Metropolitan of Arles, and a relative of his), Lupus of Troyes (Hilarius of Arles' brother-in-law), and Faustus of Riez (see Chapter 3).

More information about the foundation and influence of these early monasteries, and the final flowering of Latin culture in Gaul at this time, can be found in N. K. Chadwick's *Poetry and Letters in Early Christian Gaul* (see Bibliography).

14) St John Cassian (in his *First Book on the Incarnation of the Lord, against Nestorius*) states that a form of Pelagianism was preached in Gaul by Leoporius

of Trêves. He was condemned by Gaulish bishops, and departed for Africa. In 425, however, Augustine convinced him of his error, and he recanted. He was present at the election of Eraclius to succeed Augustine in 426, and was still living when St John Cassian was writing his First Book shortly before 430.

15) The Tradition includes the Scriptures, of course, and a great body of records, commentaries and interpretations which have stood the test of time, and witness to the Truth. The Scriptures are perfect and sufficient in themselves, but open to interpretation according to whim: the remainder of the Tradition safeguards against that. It's very ancient: indeed, some parts of it are older than the Gospels, as Christ Himself left no writings. It was against this background of verbal transmission that the Evangelists, St Paul and others composed their works. The present New Testament did not coalesce before the end of the third century, at the earliest.

16) As expressed in Chapter 26, Section 69 of Vincent of Lérins' *Commonitory*, John Cassian's *Third Conference of Abbot Chaeremon*, and Chapters 11 – 18 and 33 of his *Institutes*. The danger of Predestination, in their view, was that it leads to a belief that Christ died for the pre-elected only, and not for all: and is a species of fatalism. Augustine was a creative genius, with a sharp, logical mind. Like Pelagius, he had studied law, and his theorizing regarding Predestination shows as

much. In this case, however, his laudable eagerness to defend the Faith was hampered by unfortunate gaps in his knowledge of history, and what the Church in the East would perceive as an imperfect grip on theology. Homer nods.

In the end, even Blessèd Augustine's remarkable character and enormous authority were not enough to ensure universal acceptance of all the implications of his theories. They were never "Catholic", and Total Predestination is today confined to peripheral sects. Despite this slip on his part, some among the Orthodox recognize the greatness of Blessèd Augustine, and number him among the Fathers of the Church. Others see him as father of the disastrous schism between "Western" and "Eastern" Christianity.

Strangely enough in the context of St Germanus' influence, it was a Celt who was foremost in the revival of "Semi-pelagianism" in the west, he being John Duns Scotus (c.1266 – 8.11.1308), a member of the Franciscan Order. His followers, the "Scotists", and the Franciscans in general were prominent supporters of "Semi- pelagianism", as were the Jesuits. The victory of "Semi-pelagianism" in the Roman Catholic Church was sealed by the Vatican Council of 1870.

17) John Morris (1977) draws attention to the lack of connection between the Church and the poor during that period, in the western part of the Empire, at least. Exceptions mentioned by him are

Martin of Tours, Salvian of Marseilles (another of the "Massilians"), and Germanus of Auxerre: and he maintains that the only Christian authors of that age who show interest in the political influence of the poor on the government are those of Britain. This need not be attributed to Pelagianism, because other "Massilians" were famous in their day for their sympathy with the poor and needy, interpreting the Gospel in a more humanitarian way than was usual at that time.

18) Ussher (based, he says, on an ancient, anonymous work written 900 years before he saw it in the Cottonian collection) states that Germanus and Lupus received the *cursus Gallorum* (the order of Divine Service according to Gaulish practice) from St John Cassian and the "Massilians", and that these two saints brought it with them to Britain. He may have had Cotton Nero A II (an 8th-century manuscript, probably written by an Irish author in France) in mind, or some other document from that collection which may have been lost when a sizeable part of the Cottonian Library went up in flames in 1731 (see Chapter 5, Patrick).

19) As the *Gaulish Chronicle of 452* tends to praise John Cassian and censure Augustine, and includes a number of references to the lower Rhône Valley (especially Valence), is has been suggested that the author was of the Massilian circle, if not Fastidius himself.

20) Orthodox Christians would not deny for a

moment that we're all entirely dependent on God's Grace, but neither would we claim that Grace is subject to restrictive definitions. Nor would we attempt to justify the supremacy of Grace over good works by selective quotation (of Romans 11:6, for instance) out of the context of the remainder of the Scriptures and the entire Tradition. If justification through Grace alone means denying the possibility that human activity can rise up towards God and partake of Grace, then the Christian experience itself is lost. Grace, to the individual Orthodox Christian, is the entirety of God's plan for him or her, according to his or her needs, and including both thoughts and works. Proceeding according to that plan closes the gap between Grace and good works.

As Metropolitan Kallistos Ware says:

> "We hold in balance two complementary truths: without God we *can* do nothing; but without our voluntary co-operation God *will* do nothing. 'The will of man is an essential condition, for without it God does nothing' (The Homilies of St Macarius). Our salvation results from the convergence of two factors, unequal in value yet both indispensable: divine initiative and human response. What God does is incomparably the more important, but man's participation is also required".

George, Igoumen of the Monastery of Osios

Gregorios on Mount Athos, stresses the indispensibility of Grace to a somewhat greater degree:

"This is because the Grace of God is that [sic] saves us and not our own good deeds. The pharisaical self-justification has no similarity to the humble, Orthodox Christian morals. As Saint Seraphim of Sarov taught, our good deeds are not only a presupposition [sic] in order for us to receive the Grace of God, but they are also fruit of the Grace of God. However, good deeds can never become the goals of Christian life. The goal is the acquisition of Divine Grace".

21) Wade-Evans, 1944-45.

22) Victricius writes: "..if I've gone to Britain, if I've stayed there, it is in order to fulfil your commands. The bishops, my brothers in the priesthood, called upon me to make peace there. Could I, your soldier, refuse?" (*De Laude Sanctorum*).

23) For the year 431: *Ad Scottos in Christus credentes ordinatus a papa Caelestino Palladius primus episcopus mittitur*. Whether in Britain or Ireland, these "Scotti" (i.e. Irish) were Christians. Pope Caelestinus wasn't one to tolerate heresy: he exiled Caelestius the Pelagian from Italy, and was equally hard on the Nestorians. Perhaps Palladius was no ordinary deacon, but Deacon of Rome: a cleric of some standing. Archbishop Ussher (see

Chapter 5), based on an old document available to him in the 17ᵗʰ century, claims that Palladius was from Britain: but that source is apparently no longer extant, and given that Ussher was set on exalting the lineage of Anglicanism in Ireland at the expense of Roman Catholicism, one cannot now tell whether his assertion has substance.

A possibility raised by Wood is that some bishops of Gaul had agreed to send Germanus and Lupus to Britain, and that Palladius had secured the Pope's seal of approval on their decision. Wood's other suggestion is that Germanus, following his first visit, had prepared a report regarding the dangers faced by Britain's Christians, including Irish attacks: and that the Church in Rome had attempted to oppose the threat by christianizing these enemies. If so, it would testify to the Church's leaders' determination to retain control on the furthest limits of their influence, despite (or because of) the civil Empire's inability to accomplish that at the time.

24) Chadwick (1954) suggests that this Palladius could, possibly, be a relative of Rutilius Namatianus (see note 13 above). The poet describes how his young kinsman of that name left Gaul to study law in Rome *c.* 419. This Palladius' father was none other than the Exuperantius who supressed an uprising in Armorica (see Chapter 1, note 23). Exuperantius was assassinated in Arles in 424, and Chadwick conjectures that he may have been succeeded as

ducatus culmen by Germanus himself, prior to his elevation to the bishopric. This would go some way to explaining Germanus' dealings with both the rebellious Armoricans and a perceived security threat in Britain, directly opposite his Command.

25) Again, this "argument from silence" is perilous, and it is possible that Gildas had Pelagianism in mind when writing, in Chapter 12 of *De Excidio*, that: "...the Arian unbelief, fierce as a serpent spewing upon us its foreign poison, caused deadly separation between brethren dwelling together. Thus, as if a path were made across the ocean, all kinds of wild beasts began, with horrid mouths, to inject the fatal poison of every manner of heresy, and to inflict the lethal wounds of their teeth...". This particular passage is echoed in Rhygyfarch's *Vita S.Dauid*, with explicit reference to Pelagianism (see Appendix I, David and Germanus). That Arianism and other heresies did not make much headway in Britain, *pace* Gildas, is suggested by Hilary and the other Doctors already alluded to.

Quite where Gildas wrote *De Excidio* is not now known. One may presume he was within hailing distance of the chieftains he castigates, but beyond their reach. The 10th/11th Century Breton composer of his *Vita* states that Gildas was born at Arecluta, which has been taken to be Strathclyde: but Breeze draws attention to Arclid, near Sandbach in Cheshire.

26) See Dumville. Bearing in mind what we know of Germanus' connection with Powys, it is interesting that the scribal colophon to the Paris and Salisbury MSS of Pelagius' *Commentary* indicate that they may be derived from a copy written by "Meirion, disciple (?) of Peibio, in the year after the death of the two kings, Elise and Selyf". All four names are Brittonic, and the names Elise and Selyf are most consistently found amongst members of the linked ruling dynasties of Powys and Brycheiniog.

27) Morris (1965) goes too far in detecting the influence of radical Pelagianism on saints such as David of Wales and Samson, e.g. in their rejection of all worldly wealth, their alleged lack of awareness of the problem of original sin, and the lack of reverence shown by some saints towards secular and ecclesiastical authority.

28) In this context, Myres (1960) says that:

> "...in the 4th century monks were individual *sancti*, leading monastic lives in their own houses. First Eusebius of Vercelli....Martin of Tours, Amator, and Germanus of Auxerre encouraged the clerics of their cathedrals to take monastic vows, leading dedicated lives in view of their congregations; and establishing schools on the basis of their monastic clergy."

Is there not room to suppose that Germanus and

Lupus' visit persuaded the leaders of the Church in Britain that they could face and survive the dire circumstances of the time by including monastic elements in "secular" church life, as above? The urban centres where bishops sat had been in decline since the end of the fourth century: and when we next catch sight of the Church here a century or two later, in western Britain, at least, we find monastic influence very strong upon her, though it's obvious that territorial dioceses were still extant.

5. Germanus: a Constellation of Saints

Such was Germanus' fame, and so popular and influential was his biography, that it's no surprise to find him mentioned in the *Lives* of other, later saints. As O'Loughlin says:

"There is a tendency in hagiography to bring saints into alliances with other saints and present them as supporting one another, teaching one another, and being authorised within the tradition by earlier more renowned saints...".

Similarly, Willis-Bund reflects that:

"In the Latin accounts it is from St. Germanus that all the Welsh saints derive their authority, and their connection with him is always worked out with such care and detail that there is some difficulty in disproving it...There is little doubt now that the supposed advantages that would follow from being connected with the Saint led the Welsh in early times to admit a connection with him that is wholly unreal..."

Hagiographers have been eager to involve Germanus, the subject of an early and authoritative *Vita*, in the promotion of other saints, to the benefit of churches and places connected with them. This may have led to crossing the boundary between truth and fabrication: but we can't now judge exactly where or when fiction submerged fact, or to what degree. Very much of the evidence these writers built upon has been lost: and besides, their attitude to "history" was very different to ours.

In their view, this world was fast spiralling down towards the Last Judgement, and their duty, in the little remaining time, was to try and interpret the events of the past in the light of the only dependable knowledge, i.e. the Tradition, including the Scriptures. To them, David, Germanus, Illtud and the others weren't so much isolated individuals as members of a divine network created for a common purpose. They were expected to share the same characteristics, and stand togther in the light of divine Grace.

The *Life of St Samson* (one of the earliest "Lives" of a British saint, composed about the year 610), states that he was appointed abbot of a monastery in Britain founded, "it is said", by Germanus, and apparently near the Severn. The biographer was careful enough to note some uncertainty, but this is a 7th century record that Germanus was then remembered as a founder and supporter of monasticism (see Chapter 6, "Bedd Garmon", Abbey Cwm Hir; and Chapter 4, note 13).

The author of the *Book of Llandaff* (*c*.1120-1140) states that St Dyfrig was made *summus doctor* and bishop by St Germanus. Benedict of Gloucester names Germanus and Lupus as teachers of Dyfrig, but the basis for his claim is no longer known. According to the Book of Llandaff, Dyfrig taught Teilo and Samson. According to the Life of Teilo (*Vita Sancti Teliavi Episcopi*) by Geoffrey, brother of Urban, Bishop of Llandaff, (+ 1133), Teilo was taught by Dyfrig and Paulinus.

According to Ussher:

> "In the book of Llandaff...we read that Germanus
> and Lupus ordained St Dyfrig foremost instructor
> of the southern part of Britain [*dextralis partis
> Britanniæ*], chosen by the King and all the bishops:
> and that by gift of King Mourig, the Nobility, the
> Clerics, and the People, Llandaff was allocated to
> him as Bishopric."

The *Life of St Illtud* (composed about the begining of the
12th century), and the *Book of Llandaff* version of the *Life of
St Samson* both claim that Illtud was a disciple of
Germanus' in Paris, and that Illtud in turn taught
Paulinus, Samson, Gildas, David and other saints (see
below). The *Life of St Paul Aurelian* (written by Urmonoc
in 884) similarly claims that Paulinus and David sat at
Illtud's feet.

If that opinion is true which holds that Dyfrig lived
between about 425 and 505 (and it's a big "if"), and if
Germanus revisited Britain in either 445, 447, or 448
rather than in 437, it's possible that the young Dyfrig
could have come under Germanus' direct influence, or at
least that the Church Dyfrig knew bore Germanus' recent
impression. Dyfrig could then have passed that influence
on to his pupils: but as Illtud died in 537, Gildas in 570,
and Paul Aurelian about the year 573, we may safely rule
out and direct personal contact between Germanus and
those three.

According to Fenn, it may be that these saints'
hagiographers' desire to claim links with Germanus

reveals an attempt on the part of Welsh clerics to stress their orthodoxy, and thus verify and safeguard their own ecclesiastical independence from the growing power and influence of Canterbury in the 7th and 8th century.

Lupus

Lupus was Bishop of Troyes (Trecassina), a city some 60 kilometres north-east of Auxerre. He was born in Toul about the year 383 (or 395, according to Ewig), a son of the noble Epirichius. The *Vita Sancti Lupi* claims that he was Germanus' nephew, his sister's son. It's commonly supposed – following Krusch, perhaps – that Lupus' *Life* is of no historical value, being written in the 8th century in support of the Dioceses of Troyes' interests. Wood, however, maintains that it contains early elements, and Ewig is of the same opinion.

His *Life* states that Lupus married Pimeniola, sister of St Hilarius of Arles (see Chapter 1, note 15; and Chapter 4, note 9), about the year 418. He retired to Lérins for a year in 425, and was there a disciple of St Honoratus. Deciding to remain there as a monk, he went to Mâcon in 426 to sell an estate of his, and share the money out to almshouses. There he met a deputation from the church at Troyes, who informed him that Ursus, bishop of that city, had died: and the he, Lupus had been chosen to succeed him. Lupus tried to refuse the honour, but eventually compromised by accepting elevation, whilst continuing, like Germanus, to lead an ascetic life. He shepherded his flock for 52 years. He may have spent time in Brittany, for the church of Lanloup is found at Goelo, and several chapels were consecrated in his name. A carving of him can be seen at the church of Pontrieux. A parish of Saint-

Loup is also found near Auxerre.

In order to save Troyes from Atilla the Hun in 451, he was obliged to offer himself hostage, and accompany Atilla on his rampage. Following Aëtius' defeat of the Huns at Châlons, Atilla required Lupus to accompany him as far as the Rhine, believing that the bishop's presence would safeguard both him and his tribe. This led to Lupus' being accused by the Romans of aiding Atilla's escape, and he was forbidden to return to Troyes, which now stood empty, its people having fled the Huns. According to the text of the *Life* published by Krusch, Lupus attempted to regather his flock on the defensible hill (an old hillfort, perhaps) of Mont Lassois (by Vix-St Marcel, Côte d'Or), some distance from Troyes: but the attempt came to nothing, and within two years Lupus returned to Mâcon. If he no longer had an estate there, he surely had friends.

He had disciples also, and his *Life* names Polychronius of Verdun, Severus of Trier, and Albinus of Châlons. He is said to have persuaded Gebavultus, King of the Alemanii in 469/70 to release prisoners taken from Troyes: but a very similar feat is also attributed to Saint Severinus of Passau, so this may be a borrowed element. It's interesting that the *Life* of Lupus, like that of Germanus, moves quickly from the journey to Britain in 429 to having to face a powerful "barbarian" ruler, and succeeding in diverting him from his destructive intentions.

Many miracles are attributed to Lupus, including healing the sick and reviving the dead. He is said to have spent his church's treasure on aiding the poor and freeing the enslaved.

He died to this world in 479, was initially buried at St Martin's church in Areis, and subsequently outside the walls of Troyes. Then his remains were transferred to two handsome reliquaries. His feast day is kept on July the 29th. Sidonius Apollinaris (see Chapter 2) held Lupus' literary taste and eloquence in high regard, calling him "father of fathers, bishop of bishops, prince of the Gaulish prelates, column of virtue, friend of God". In approbation of Annianus, Bishop of Orlèans, Sidonius states that he is "equal to Lupus" and "not unequal to Germanus": praise indeed.

"Lupus" is translated "Bleiddian" in Welsh, but identification of a church of "Llanfleiddian" near Cowbridge ("Llanfleiddian Fawr", as Iolo Morgannwg (Edward Williams) would have it) relates to a more recent individual named Elyddan or Elyddon, not the Lupus of Troyes. Baring-Gould and Fisher state that the "Llanfleiddian Fach" near Cardiff is properly "Llanelyddon", and Bartrum gives "Llwyneliddon" as the correct name of that village. Either way, St Lupus is not involved.

Brieuc (Briog, Briocus)

According to the *Life* of St Brieuc (written before the year 850), he was sent, at ten years of age, to be educated by Germanus at Paris. Patrick and Illtud were his fellow-pupils, and he remained there until ordained priest. In the version published in *Analecta Bollandiana ii* (1883), Germanus came from Ireland to Ceredigion, where he met the Irish chieftain Cuerp and Eldruda his Saxon wife.

They presented their child, Brieuc (Welsh, "Briog") to Germanus' care, and both saints then journeyed to Paris.

Camille, Magnance, and Pallaye

It is recorded that the parish churches of Escolives-Sainte Camille, Sainte Magnance, and Sainte Pallaye in the vicinity of Auxerre were founded by three women who accompanied Germanus' remains from Ravenna to Auxerre.

Ciarán

In the Latin "Life" of St Ciarán, Bishop of Ossory and founder of Saighir (who died c.530 AD), a *quidam religiosus peregrinus nomine Germanus* (wanderer/stranger/ pilgrim named Germanus) is named, and it is mentioned that Ciarán had a bell made *apud Germanum episcopum, magistrum Sancti Patricii* (by/in the presence of/in the dwelling of Bishop Germanus, teacher of St Patrick). In his Gaelic *Life*, however, it is said that the bell was wrought *doroine Gaerman gabha do grasaibh De* (by German the smith, by the Grace of God).

David of Wales

See Appendix I, "David and Germanus".

Geneviève

According to the *Vita Genouefae*, there was a direct connection between that saint (422-512) and St Germanus of Auxerre, as follows:

On the first journey to Britain, Germanus and Lupus stayed at Nanterre. As the inhabitants flocked to hear them preach, Germanus took special note of Geneviève, though she was but seven years old. Following the sermon, he told her parents that he foresaw she would be a saint; that she would realize her ambition to serve God, and that others would follow her example. When he asked Geneviève if she would like to serve God in perpetual virginity, and bear the title of Bride of Christ, she replied that that was her long-held desire, and begged his blessing, so that she would be consecrated unto God from that moment forth. Germanus went to the local church, and during the Ninth Hour and Vespers, he placed his hand upon her head. Afterwards, following a meal, he returned her to her parents, commanding them to bring her to him early the following morning.

So it came to pass: and when Germanus asked her whether she remembered the promise she had made to God, she replied that she did, and would attempt to keep it, with divine help. Germanus gave her a bronze medallion with a cross thereon, to hang perpetually about her neck, to remind her of her consecration unto God. At the same time he charged her never to wear bracelets, beads, or any other vain adornments. She obeyed utterly.

Years later she was accused of being a visionary, a hypocrite, and unchaste. Germanus' second visit to Paris silenced her critics for a while, but they soon went on the attack again, and it was decided that she should be drowned. Then the Archdeacon of Auxerre arrived, bearing to her a gift from the hand of Germanus himself: bread consecrated by him, as a sign of his great respect for her virtues, and of communion with her.[1] That was enough to convince or silence her critics, and the prejudice against her turned to deep respect all the rest of

136

her earthly life.

It has been suggested that the *Life of St Geneviève* was written by a priest who was acquainted with her, during the reign Childebert, King of the Franks (511-558). However, it is generally thought to be largely fictional, and to date from the time of Charlemagne. Wood holds that it is based on a sixth-century work, which could contain ancient factual details. For example, that Germanus' second visit to Paris is connected with his second visit to Britain.

Patrick

St Patrick is known to have written two surviving texts: his *Confession* and his *Letter to Coroticus*. He makes no mention of either Germanus or Palladius, and there is no evidence that he ever met Germanus, or was ever on the Continent. He does mention (in his *Confession*) that he would like to visit Gaul if the opportunity arose: implying that he hadn't already done so, even though his mission was plainly very advanced. And, though mindful of the perils of "arguing from silence", it's to be remarked that Patrick's writings mention neither Germanus, Palladius, nor any other such figure, when to have done so would have bolstered his case against his critics.

The quality of Patrick's Latin is as could be expected of one who had spent time in late Roman northern or central Gaul: but the culture of contemporary southern and eastern Roman Britain was very similar to that of northern Gaul, in both content and quality (see Chapter 3, note 9). The *Confession* and *Letter* employ phraseology and devices current in contemporary continental works, which could indicate that teachers of rhetoric fleeing the collapse of Roman Gaul sought safety and employment in the Britain of Patrick's youth. There is, in short, no sound evidence that Patrick ever set foot on the European continent.

Sometime after 664-668 Tirechan edited a collection of notes regarding Patrick. He gives two versions of his *Life*, one stating that the saint escaped from Ireland and spent thirty years on one of the islands of "Aralanensis". A corruption, perhaps of the Isles of Lérins in the Diocese of Arles (see Chapter 4), or of "Lerinsis" (Latin "from Lérins"). No mention is made of Germanus.

One of the many later additions to Tirechan's notes states that Patrick and Isernus were with Germanus in Auxerre, when Germanus told Iserninus that he should preach in Ireland. He replied that he was ready to obey and preach anywhere other than that island, whereupon Germanus turned to Patrick, and said "And you: will you be obedient?" Patrick replied, "Let it be as you wish". Germanus said, "Let this be between you. Eventually, Isernus will not be able to avoid going to Ireland". The source of this account is unknown. The *Chronicon Scottorum* and *Annals of Inisfallen* state that Iserninus arrived in Ireland in the year 438.

Muirchú, who composed a *Life of St Patrick* c.690, says nothing of "Aralanensis" or "Isles of the Tyrrhenian Sea", but states that Ireland's patron saint was a pupil of Germanus' in Auxerre, and that Germanus sent Patrick and Segetius to Rome. On the way there, they heard from St Augustine and St Benedict about Palladius'

138

unsuccessful mission in Ireland, and of his death in Britain. The local bishop, "Amathorex", ordained Patrick bishop on the spot: and rather than proceed to Rome, Patrick went to Ireland. It is known that Augustine of Hippo lived from 354 to 430, and Benedict of Nursia *c*.480 - *c*.540.

Fiacc's Hymn to St Patrick (7th – 8th century, probably) contains the following:

"....His path across the wondrous sea, Until he stayed with Germanus in the south, In the south of Lethia. In the isles of the Tyrrhenian Sea he sojourned, There he studied. He read the canon with Germanus, According to history [*or:* writings]..."

The Book of Armagh (9th century) contains the *Sayings of Patrick*, claimed to be three quotations of the saint's own words. The first states:

"On my journeys through the provinces of Gaul, through Italy and even among the islands of the Tyrrhenian Sea, the fear of God was my guide".

As the second quoted *Saying* is from the *Letter to Coroticus*, and there is nothing in the third to suggest a date later than Patrick's own period, at least one author has suggested that the *Sayings* are genuine, and are one of the sources used by Muirchú when composing Patrick's *Life*.

Tirechan, Fiacc and Muirchú seem to have access to a source or sources other than Constantius' *Life*. Constantius writes nothing of Lérins, but Tirechan and

Fiacc seem aware of a connection with that area. Constantius doesn't mention Amator, Germanus' predecessor as Bishop of Auxerre, but Muirchú states that a bishop named "Amathorex" is connected with Germanus, and includes him in a tale which plugs an unwelcome gap in St Patrick's life history with an account of a visit to Auxerre.

Fiacc's (and the *Sayings'*) reference to "the south of Lethia" and the "isles of the Tyrrhenian Sea", may indicate awareness of Germanus' relations with noted clerics connected to that particular monastery, or at least with the "Massilians" of the Rhône-Provence region in general (see Chapter 3). Sidonius certainly implies that written works could pass directly from thence to the far West, and the Irish authors could well have derived material from such a work, using it to exalt St Patrick.

They do not seem to have been aware of the cycle of Germanus legends employed by Nennius: but Nennius may well have had access to a version of whatever source was used by Muirchú, for in Chapter 51 of his *Historia* he writes:

"The death of Palladius being known, the Roman patricians, Theodosius and Valentinian, then reigning, Pope Celestine sent Patrick to convert the Scots to the faith of the Holy Trinity; Victor, the angel of God, accompanying, admonishing, and assisting him, and also the bishop Germanus. Germanus then sent the ancient Segerus with him as a venerable and praiseworthy bishop, to King Amatheus [*or in another MS:* ...the elder Segerus with him to a wonderful man, the holy bishop

140

Amathearex], a who lived near, and who had prescience of what was to happen; he was consecrated bishop in the reign of that king by the holy pontiff [or *in other MSS:* ...received the episcopal degree from the holy bishop Amatheorex / ...received the episcopal degree from Matheorex and the holy bishop], assuming the name of Patrick, having hitherto been known by that of Maun; Auxilius, Isserninus, and other brothers were ordained with him to inferior degrees"

Later versions of the "Life of St Patrick", up to (and including) that of Jocelyn of Furness *c.*1185, only add further characters and locations to the above. The name of one purported site, "Mount Arnon" in the Tyrrhenian Sea, rather resembles to Germanus' name in Welsh, "Garmon".

In Bibliothèque National (Paris) MS lat. 17294, a work of the early 15th century, the first breviary lesson for the Feast of St David reads as follows:

Cum sanctus Germanus predicaret in Britannia contra heresum Pelagiam, iam beatum Patriciun sibi ad familiare contubernium sociauit.

"While St Germanus was preaching in Britain against the Pelagian heresy, he admitted St Patrick into his fellowship."[2]

Thus whoever composed the lesson was convinced of a close connection between Germanus and Patrick, but had them meet in Britain, not on the Continent. In a miniature at the lower left-hand corner of folio 426v. of the

141

manuscript, St Germanus is depicted as a mitred bishop, with Patrick seated beside him. Another miniature in the lower right-hand corner of the same page shows Germanus and Patrick reading in a walled garden at Vallis Rosina (Menevia).

Authors have tried to reconcile these accounts of a relationship between Patrick and Germanus by postulating that there were two Germani, two Patricks, or that they were kin. The available evidence does not support such theories. The period of Patrick's life is a subject of debate, and later Irish annals give differing dates for his mission and death. Opinion, on the whole, inclines to believe that he was active during the second half of the 5th century, and that the record of his death in 493 may be correct. It is very unlikely that he had direct contact with Germanus.

According to Ussher:

> "Regarding the form of the liturgy, or the public service of God, which St Patrick bought to this land [Ireland]: it is said that he received it from Germanus and Lupus; and that it came originally from St Mark the Evangelist. For so I saw recorded in an old fragment, written quite 900 years ago, which now remains in the library of my worthy friend, Sir Robert Coton;"

This "fragment" is doubtless the "booklet" Ussher refers to again in claiming that Germanus and Lupus bought the text of the Gallican Mass to Britain (see Chapter 4, note 13).

142

According to Nankivell, some inhabitants of Auxerre liked to believe that an ancient fresco "by Germanus' relics" [sic] depict St Germanus blessing St Patrick. He does not say where these relics are.

Peris.

A letter from "G. R." to Edward Lhuyd (probably c.1700) records a legend which attempts to explain the presence of Arctic char (known locally as *torgoch*, pl *torgochiaid*) in the lakes of Llyn Peris, Llyn Cwellyn and Llyn Dulyn in Gwynedd, Wales. The Latin of the letter is rather obscure, but it seems that the belief was that St Peris had given some of the least of the char in his lake to St Germanus. Germanus had then introduced the larger of them into Llyn Cwellyn (in the parish of Betws Garmon), and gave the least to St Rhedyw (see below). Rhedyw then introduced them into the waters of Llyn Dulyn, in the parish of Llanllyfni: and this explains why the char of Llyn Cwellyn are larger than those of Llyn Dulyn, but those of Llyn Peris are largest of all (see Chapter 8).

Rhedyw

In W. R. Ambrose's *Hynafiaethau, Cofiannau a Hanes Presennol Nant Nantlle* (1872) we find on pages 16 – 17:

"Llanllyfni Church is consecrated to Saint Rhedyw, or Rhedicus, who blossomed about the year 316AD. ...if reports are to be at all believed...at one period of his life he held a high position in the church at Augustodunum (Autun). His name is well known as a famous writer, because he took a prominent part in the debate about the heresy of Arius of Alexandria...He was also father of

Garmon, or Germanus, the hero of the famous battle of Maes Gaermon [sic]."

That Rhedyw was ever in Gaul or took any part in the debate concerning Arianism has no basis in any known text or plausible tradition. The claim that Germanus was a son of a "Ridicus" is recorded by Edward Lhuyd: and it may be conjectured that both ideas spring from an elaborated version of St Germanus' Vita in which it was said that his father's name was Rusticus (see Chapter 8).

Ninnocha (Gwengwystl\Gwengu\Gwen).

The *Life* of this saint (in the Cartullary of Quimperlé, ed. P. de Berthou, Paris 1896) claims that Patrick sent Germanus to Brycheiniog (*ad Brochanum regem Britanniae*), i.e. the upper Usk Valley, now in Powys, Wales.

Notes.

1. Cf. his gift of bread to the Empress Placidia (Chapter 1).

2. Edwards, O. T., pp. 244-245.

Plate 1. St Germanus heals Volusianus' son. Stained glass of c.1230-40, window 10, ambulatory of St Stephen's Cathedral, Auxerre.

Plate 2. St Germanus gives his money to the poor. Stained glass of c.1230-40, window 10, ambulatory of St Stephen's Cathedral, Auxerre.

Plate 3. St Germanus heals Elafius' son. Stained glass of c.1230-40, window 10, ambulatory of St Stephen's Cathedral, Auxerre.

Plate 4: St Germanus. Stained glass of c.1350, window 40, south transept of St Stephen's Cathedral, Auxerre.

Plate 5. St Germanus. 13th Century stone image at the church of Saint-Germain-l'Auxerrois, Paris.

6. Locations Connected with St Germanus

The following are dedications in St Germanus of Auxerre's name, or sites otherwise connected with him.

In Wales:

St Germanus of Auxerre is widely known in Wales as Garmon Sant, and mediaeval Welsh ecclesiastical calendars give several dates for his feast days, including May the 27th and 28th, July the 13th, 14th, 30th and 31st, and October the 1st. Germanus slept in the Lord on July the 31st, and his relics were translated on October the 1st: the other dates are proper to a different saint, Germanus of Paris. Both being of the same name, there has obviously been some confusion.

The number of dedications in St Germanus' name in north Wales was (and is) taken by some as evidence of the saint's missionary and military campaign during his first visit to Britain. D. R. Thomas, for instance, stated that the Roman road known as "Sarn Sws":

"...leads from Caersws, and crossing the hills near Llanerfyl and Llanfihangel skirts the Berwyns from Llanrhaiadr to Llanarmon, and passing on hence to Glyndyfrdwy wends towards Iâl and Caergwrle (qu. Bovium), and thence to Chester (Deva). This is the line which the holy Garmon (S. Germanus) must have followed as he planted the churches that still hand down his name in Mechain and Mochnant (Llananrmon Mynydd mawr), in Dyffryn Ceiriog and Iâl, and when he crowned his mission with the great Halleluiatic [sic]

150

victory at Maes Garmon, Mold."

E. G. Bowen did draw attention to the incidence of saints' dedications and known routeways in Wales, including Roman roads. However, to deduce the presence of a road from the present distribution of known Germanus dedications is much more speculative. To further declare that Germanus "must" have followed that route on a military campaign, or even that he was ever physically present at those places, is most presumptive. As in the case of constellations, it's tempting to join up the dots and make them depict what we'd like to see. All that can be said for certain is that many of the Germanus dedications in Wales are in the old realm of Powys, with outliers in the Conwy valley and, broadly, western Snowdonia.

To the individual dedications:

Llanarmon, Eifionydd, Gwynedd. A church (formerly a chapel in the parish of Llangybi) possessing *Cloch Garmon,* a "Celtic" handbell of bronze with an iron clapper. This is depicted in "H.H."'s leaflet, *Eglwysi Llangybi a Llanarmon,* and I believe it to be the one shown on page 64 of John and Rees (see Bibliography). Llanarmon Eifionydd stands not far distant from Nant Gwrtheyrn and Gwynnys, scene of one version of Vortigern's cataclysmic demise.

Betws Garmon, "Germanus' Oratory", Arfon, Gwynedd. A church and holy well. According to a manuscript of one Dafydd Pritchard (1964) quoted by J. O. Huws:

"The Betws here was established by Saint Germanus in the times of the Crusades...Tradition says that the old

Betws was up on the slope of Hafod y Wern. The purpose of establishing the Betws here was to have a resting-place, and to have succour on their journey whilst carrying the body of some saint or other to Bardsey for burial. And then, on returning, to pray for his soul which was in purgatory for some period of time or other. As far as I know, there's no record of what was carried on here, nor of who cared for the place."

A somewhat vague account, admittedly, but correct in stating that the ruins of an old chapel are to be found near St Germanus' Well at Hafod y Wern, about a mile west of the present church, and near a track westward across the pass between Mynydd Mawr and Moel Tryfan. The Abbey of the Mother of God on Bardsey Island (*Ynys Enlli*) was a renowned place of pilgrimage, and burial there, amongst a reputed throng of 20,000 saints, was supposedly a passport to Paradise.

Cwm Garmon. "Germanus' Valley" in the parish of Llangower, Penllyn, Gwynedd.

Capel Garmon, "Germanus' Chapel", Llanrwst, Conwy. A church and holy well. The township of Garth Garmon and the site of Pall Garmon (see Chapter 8) are both nearby. Lhuyd's *Parochialia* records that the chapel was built by Dafydd Anwyl ap Ieuan ap Rhys of Plas yn Rhos in the titheland named Garth Garmon on the banks of the River Hwch.

(Aber) Ffynnon Armon, Colion / Clocaenog, Denbighshire. This holy well is mentioned in the Bachymbyd MSS, and as "Craig Ffynnon Armon" (Buddugre'r Iarll) in the town

records of Ruthin. In 1699 Edward Lhuyd recorded "Fynnon Armon in Bodhigre'r Iarlh formerly much frequented".

Maes Garmon, "Germanus' Field", Mold, Flintshire. The site of the Hallelujah Victory, according to a tradition first recorded by Ussher in 1639:

In agro Flintensi, iuxta oppidum quod Angli Mold Cambrobritanni Guid-cruc appellant, hoc gestum aiunt; indeq, locum Maes Garmon...

A memorial obelisk was erected on the site by Nehemiah Griffith of Rhual, Mold in 1736.

Bryngarmon, "Germanus' Hill", Mold, Flintshire.

Erw Armon, "Germanus' Acre", Dinhinlle, Wrexham. An area of land near Ruabon: "Manerium de Isgoed. Dinhinlle. Johannes Eyton gen' tenet...17, Erw Armon, continen' dimid' acre;".

Dryll Garmon, "Germanus' Quillet", Rhiwlas, Chirk, Wrexham. A site noted in a Chirk Castle MSS of 1626.

Llanarmon yn Iâl, Wrexam. A church. John Leland (c.1536-39) states that Llanarmon and Llandegla were the foremost parishes of the Lordship of Bromfield (*Maelor Gymraeg*), adding:

"Greate pilgremage and offering was a late to S. Armon".

Edward Lhuyd recorded the existence of a carved image

of St Germanus there on 11.10.1671 (see Chapter 8). According to the *Valor Ecclesiasticus* of 1535, the total value of the offerings before the "Ymage of Saint Germo'" was £4 and 10 shillings. This could refer to the image on the south wall of the church, or to another, now lost.

E. O. Williams had it that the church "...is believed to commemorate the spot where the Easter festival was solemnized by the bishop in the wattled fabric" prior to the Hallelujah Victory.

There's at least one well, if not two, dedicated in St Germanus' name in this parish. A *Craig Ffynnon Armon* ("The rock of Germanus' Well") (1589/90) and *Brynie Ffynnon Armon* (The Hills of Germanus' Well") (1650) are noted in Ruthin town records as being in Llanarmon yn Iâl. A well at a place known as "The Saint's Crossing" is listed in the Royal Commission on Ancient Monuments' list of Denbighshire antiquities, and the Tithe Schedule names a *Cae'r Saint* (Saints' Field) thereabouts.[1] It is by Bryniau Ffynnon Armon, on the boundary with the parish of Llandegla (Ordnance Survey Grid Ref. SH195523).

It has been recently claimed that another well has been uncovered below the parish church, nearer to the River Alyn (OSGR SH193563). There was a township of Llanarmon (Tre'r Llan) in the parish and, according to the Extent Book of 1778, two quillets of land named *Tir y Saint* ("The Saints' Land") in the township of *Gwaun y Ffynnon* ("Well Moor").

Llanarmon yn Iâl Fair was celebrated on the 1st of August,

the day after the patronal feast. *Ffair y Bol* (the "Belly Fair", where nothing but food was sold) was held on the preceding Saturday. Two references in the wardens' accounts to the purchase of loads of rushes (to be spread on the church floor, likely) in August 1763 may suggest that the church was cleaned in time for the feast, or immediately afterwards. St Germanus and the Hallelujah Victory are depicted in the west window of the south aisle.

Prince Gruffydd ap Cynan left ten shillings in his will to "lan Armawn", probably Llanarmon yn Iâl, where Owain Gwynedd his son built an earthen castle (*Tomen y Faerdre*). This mound stands a short distance due east of the church: and bearing in mind the number of similar mounds found near churches dedicated in St Germanus' name in Wales, and called after him, one is tempted to conjecture that Owain Gwynedd may, with economy in mind, have created his fortress by building upon a pre-existing *Tomen Armon* ("Germanus' Mound"). There is, however, no proof of that.

Llanarmon Dyffryn Ceiriog, Wrexham. A church, with a *Boncyn* or *Twmpath Garmon* ("Germanus' Mound") and "a piece of glebe" named *Erw Garmon* ("Germanus' Acre") nearby. D. R. Thomas notes that "an early tradition" stated St Germanus to have been "buried under a plain stone" within the church. In 1279 Edward the 1st granted to Llywelyn ap Gruffydd of Bromfield and his heirs the right to hold a weekly market on Tuesdays at his manor of "Llanarmon in the hundred of Cynllaith in Wales", and an annual three-day fair on the feast of SS Silin and Germanus (the 1st of October).

155

Llanarmon Mynydd Mawr (Llanarmon Fach), Wrexham. A church, which was once a chapel in the parish of Llanrhaeadr ym Mochnant.

Llanarmon ym Mechain (Llanfechain), Powys. A church, with a *Tomen Armon* ("Germanus' Mound") adjacent to it on the north side, and a *Ffynnon Armon* ("Germanus' Well") 300 yards to the south at Tŷ Coch. T. A. Richards recorded in 1872 that the well was bounded by a few large stones, and overlooked by an old yew. The spring was "not copious" but "held in veneration" and occasionally used for baptisms at the church, and keeping butter cool in summer. The patronal feast was celebrated on the first Sunday following October the 12th, which would coincide with the feast of the Translation of the Relics of St Germanus (October the 1st) according to the Julian Calendar.

D. R. Thomas records the mound as *Twmpath Garmon*; speculates that Germanus "probably" preached thereon; states that baptismal water was carried from the well until the 19th century, and that the practice had been revived by the rector at the time of writing (1908 – 13).

The author "T" (D. R. Thomas again, perhaps) speculates that the Llanfechain mound, and others connected with Germanus dedications, may have been prehistoic burial mounds "utilised by the missionary in his preaching, or they may have been raised for the occasion, as seems to be implied in the case of St. David at Llanddewi Brefi in Cardiganshire".

Castle Caereinion, Powys. A church, in whose yard stands a mound which has been connected with Germanus. It may originally have been a mediaeval fortification, or a fortification may have built upon it in mediaeval times (see Llanarmon yn Iâl above). Also, a holy well. According to D. R. Thomas, a Bishop Tanner had it as dedicated to St Jerome: but more correctly, to St Germanus. The saint's festival was celebrated on the 1st of October.

Craig Llwyn Armon, Llangynog, Powys. As in the case of *Llwyn Padarn* ("Padarn's Grove"), Llanberis and *Llwyn Gwynhoedl* (Gwynhoedl's Grove"), Clynnog Uchaf, this "Rock of Germanus' Grove" could indicate an isolated, woody area in which a saint dwelt in seclusion from time to time.

Pwll Erw Armon ("The Pool of Germanus' Acre"), Llandrinio, Powys. In the Commote of Deuddwr, 1561: "...a pasture called Y borra isa...and in length from Pwll erw armon on the one end...", "...a place called pigin purgin and erw armon...".

Saint Harmons, Powys. In the commote of Gwrtheyrnion, an area connected with Vortigern and his descendants. The parish contains the settlement of Clas Garmon, indicating an important ecclesiastical community of canons under the authority of a bishop or abbot. The Manor of Clas Garmon was held by the Bishops of St Davids, and they had an estate there. Edward the 1st granted the bishop and his successors the right to hold a market there on Mondays; a three-day fair on the Feast of St Germanus, and warrenry: indicating that the manor

157

was of economic importance. Here, according to Gerald of Wales, was kept St Curig's Crozier, "which extends somewhat at its top, both on one side and the other, in the form of a cross". Such T-shaped croziers are borne by the Orthodox higher clergy to this day. The present 19th-century church has a fine stained glass window depicting St Germanus. The remains of a Roman fort lie a little south-west of the village.

Regarding the granting of land at St Harmons by Vortimer to St Germanus, see Chapter 3 (Nennius), note 10.

Bedd Garmon ("Germanus' Grave"), Abbey Cwm Hir, Powys. The Rev. Jonathan Williams, writing in 1858, stated that:

"There is also, on the bank of the river Marteg, at the eastern extremity of the parish, near to the confines of Llanbister, a remarkable and conspicuous tumulus named Bedd Garmon, *i.e.*, the grave of Garmon, where perhaps the tutelary saint of this parish, or of some person of that name of distinguished note, lies interred. Probability favours the former suggestion, as tradition has transmitted an account that St. Garmon had an hermitage adjoining to the church-yard of this parish."

The site in question lies in Abbey Cwm Hir parish, once part of Llanbister. Sadly, Williams does not give the source of the interesting information about the hermitage. It could be a recollection of the dwelling of an anchorite or hermit by the church, or of ascetics connected with Clas Garmon in the nearby parish of Saint Harmon. Cwm

Hir is but a short step from the Teme, a tributary of the Severn: and one is tempted to view this *clas* in the light of the suggestion in the *Life of St Samson* (see Chapter 5) that the monastery founded by Germanus was not far from the Severn. There is, however, no other evidence to that effect, and Samson's biographer may have had St Illtud's foundation at Llanilltud Fawr (*anglice* "Llantwit Major") in mind.

It appears that the name *Bedd Garmon* for this feature is no longer used, it now being "The Mount", according to Ordnance Survey maps. The CADW website, however, suggests that the "Mount" is *Bedd Garmon*. Having visited the site in August 2010, I found it to be indeed on the banks of Marteg, slightly south of its confluence with Nant-y-ffin ("the boundary stream"), at OS Grid Reference SO 01109 75494 and behind Maes-y-gwaelod farmhouse. It's presently no more than a round hummock a few feet high.

Doble draws attention to a megalithic monument, near St Illtud's church at Defynnog, "known as the *Bedd* or Grave of Illtyd's Festival, a very unusual type of name, showing the prominence of the liturgical observance of the saint's *depositio* in the traditions of the locality." At this site the saint "was honoured until comparatively recently by the practice, dear to the Catholic Welsh, of "watching" (vigil) before his festival." *Bedd Garmon* could well have been the focus of a similar custom, as could *Bedd Twrog* (St Twrog) in Arfon, and *Bedd Gelert* (St Geler) in Snowdonia.
Regarding Germanus' connection with another prehistoric site, see *Pall Garmon* in Chapter 8.

Ffynnon Armon \ *Iermon, Llanfihangel ar Arth*, Carmarthenshire. By *Caer Gwrtheyrn* ("Vortigern's Fort"): Erasmus Saunders, writing to Edward Lhuyd at the turn of the 18ᵗʰ century, mentions *Cerrig Gwrtherin* ("Vortigern's Rocks") in this parish. The 1917 Report of the Royal Commission on Ancient Monuments mentions:

..."Craig Gwrtheyrn Camp", and a copious and dependable spring nearby "called 'Ffynnon Garmon' or 'King Garmon's Well'. This tradition concerning the well of "King Garmon" (by whom is meant the popular saint, Germanus) connects the Gwrtheyrn of this camp with the Vortigern of fable."

"Blaen Armonth", Uwchmynydd, Colwyn, Elfael, Powys. A document of 1618:

"To the 29ᵗʰ 30ᵗʰ 31ᵗʰ Articles wee finde a parcell of landes called *Blaen Armonth* in Llansanfreed beinge in the tenure of Steephen Dunn gent...".

This could be a corruption of a place name such as "Blaenau'r Mynydd" (Heads\Upland Valleys of the Mountains): but although one wouldn't expect the soft mutation of a personal name (changing Garmon to Armon) following a masculine singular noun such as "blaen" (head \ top\ end \ upland valley), this name could, possibly, be a corruption of *Blaen Armon* ("Germanus' Valley"). Another possibility is that an interposing feminine singular noun such as "ffynnon" (well) may have been dropped from a place name originally "Blaen *Ffynnon* Armon", or suchlike.

160

Pennant Melangell, Powys. The Rev. Elias Owen, overheard speculating in 1894 about the presence of a mound near the church at Pennant Melangell, said that churches dedicated in the name of St Germanus "always had such a mound in the church-yard; and that it was said Pennant Church was dedicated to two Saints, and that two Saints' days were kept annually." He could have been conjecturing that the "second saint" was Germanus: but the presence of a mound is not, in itself, evidence of a Germanus dedication (see Appendix I).

Apart from the ancient sites above, two churches have been consecrated in St Germanus' name in more recent times. In Cardiff, at the corner of Star Street and Metal Street, Splott, stands an Anglican church in Gothic style designed by G. F. Bodley, built in 1884 on land donated by Lord Tredegar, and consecrated in 1886.

In Lôn Garmon, Abersoch, there's a Roman Catholic church dedicated in memory of St Germanus. It's open between May and September.

Brittany:

Plougastel, Kemper: a church.

Pleyben, Châteaulin: a church.

Clohars-Carnoët: a church.

Riec, Pont-aven: a church.

Cornwall:

Germanus and Petroc are often seen as joint founders of the Diocese of Cornwall. MS Bodley 572 (Bodleian Library, Oxford) contains the proper for the Mass of St Germanus (*Missa propria Germani episcopi*). It appears to be a supplementary leaflet to a sacramental (similar to a Greek *Euchologion*), rescripted in south-west Britain (if not in Cornwall itself) about the mid-10th century. In it, Germanus is termed "bishop" and "confessor", and it is stated that his relics are at *Lannaled* (present-day St Germans, Cornwall), and are visited by pilgrims from several lands and of several languages.

It reports that Germanus was sent from Rome by Pope Gregory the Great, to be the "lantern and pillar" of Cornwall [*lucerna et columna Cornubiae*]: and that he met with success at Lanaled, "wiping away the darkness and infidelity that blinded hearts and senses": Pelagianism, no doubt. The "folly and madness of unfaithful and cruel King Vortigern" is also mentioned, suggesting that the writer was familiar with Nennius' work.

The writer had some knowledge of Germanus' labours in Britain, but not of the exact details of Constantius' *Life*. He believed that Germanus was active in Cornwall, and that some of his relics were at St Germans, though he does not say that Germanus was buried there. The name of Gregory the Great may have been lifted from an account of Augustine of Canterbury's mission, but could indicate that Germanus was hazily remembered as having been sent to Britain by a pope.

Interestingly, the Greek title *archimandrita* is here used for

162

"bishop": but insular writers of that period did rather like to show off their learning by peppering their works with Greek words, and *archimandrita* occurs in several mediaeval Latin texts.

St Germans church was a monastery and, along with Bodmin, joint cathedral of the Diocese of Cornwall between 930 and 1050, after which Cornwall was assumed into the Diocese of Exeter. The *Exeter Relic List*, by Leofric first bishop of that city (from 1046 onwards) mentions *Reliquae Sancti Germani Autisiodori Episcopi.* "Reliquae" could mean an entire body, rather than a part or parts only (i.e. *reliquiis*). If there was a whole body, it wasn't Germanus', for that was at Auxerre.

If there was a relic of Germanus' at St Germans, (and the wording of the *Missa* is rather vague), then it was probably lost (at the time of the translation to Exeter, or in a Viking raid, perhaps) by 1358: for in that year other relics of the saint were brought from Auxerre to St Germans at the request of Sir Nicholas Tamworth (or Tremorze). They were an arm bone, and part of the fine silk in which the remains at Auxerre were wrapped. John Grandisson, Bishop of Exeter, placed these in a silver casket presented by Sir Nicholas, and in a letter dated 20.5.1361 granted 40 days indulgence to all who revered the relics at St Germans on July the 31st or October the 1st, or during the seven days following these feasts. Such relics may have been kept in the "episcopal tomb" (*tumbe*) Leland saw there about the year 1540. If so, he didn't record it: but did note:

"...and over the Tumbe a xi. Bisshops paynted with their

163

Names and Verses as token of so many Bisshops biried theere, or that ther had beene so many Bisshops of Cornwalle that had theyr Seate theer."

Perhaps St Germanus' image was among them.

A fair was held on St Germanus' Eve and Day by 1284, and St Germanus' Day celebrated there on July the 31st by 1340. A local fair was held on August the 1st 1602.

By 1652, the patronal feast was celebrated at St Germans at the end of May, i.e. St Germanus of Paris' Day, in addition to the 31st of July. As William Worcester (1478) notes the celebrating of St Germanus' feasts at Bodmin on May the 27th and July the 31st, and we also know that it was kept at Rame (see below) on May the 31st by 1309, one can see that the confusion between the two Saints Germanus was not confined to Wales.

Rame, Cornwall: a church.

Padstow, Cornwall: a chapel. On the 28th of September 1415 Laurence Merthere, Vicar of Padstow, was licenced to celebrate in the chapels of that parish, viz. those of the Trinity, St Michael, St Petroc, St Germanus, and St Wethenye. In 1745, the Vicar of Padstow was informed that "there were seven or eight chapels in my parish, but they are all in ruins, and the names of most entirely forgotten."

St Neot's, Cornwall: an early-16th century stained glass depiction of St Germanus in one of the church windows. Apart from Neot being one of Cornwall's foremost saints, his feast coincided with one of St Germanus', i.e. July the 31st.

The Isle of Man:

Saint Germans' Cathedral, Peel, and the nearby township of St Germans.

The *Chronicon Manniae* states that the cathedral was built by Bishop Symon, who was bishop 1227 – 1247. According to Kinvig, "Considerable confusion has been caused regarding some of the [parish] names…Similarly, the name Malew, which is derived from the Irish Mo-Lua, became mixed up with St. Lupus of Troyes, who was a very different person, and the Manx saint German with St Germanus of Auxerre, who was actually St. Patrick's teacher."

One way of attempting to reconcile all the evidence regarding Germanus, despite its varying quality, is to argue for the existence of more than one St Germanus (e.g. Baring-Gould and Fisher). The one being Bishop of Auxerre, and the other a saint who laboured further to the west, in Brittany, Cornwall, Ireland, Wales and Man. It appears that this theory is presently out of favour with the learnèd, but has continued to cast its shadow on the subject. All that may be safely said in this instance is that a thirteenth-century bishop decided to consecrate a cathedral in the name (or in memory) of a saint named Germanus: perhaps Germanus of Auxerre, or Germanus of Paris. The mention of an admittedly erroneous dedication to Lupus suggests that some were of the opinion that Germanus of Auxerre is patron saint of Peel

Cathedral.

Ireland:

Cil Gorman, Arklow: a church. As Gildas states that Saxon attacks had caused many Britons to flee abroad, some scholars allow the possibility that "abroad" could mean Ireland, as well as Brittany. Is this dedication, on the coast beside a convenient crossing point between both islands, evidence of such a link? A large hoard of Roman coins was found in a vessel buried near to this church.

Loch Garman is the Irish name of the bay called "Llwch Garmon" in the Welsh chronicle, *Brut y Tywysogion*, "Llwch Garmawn" in the *Historia Gruffud vab Kenan*, and the bay, town and county of Wexford in English. According to O'Donovan, "Dun Carman" was the name of a fort which stood on the site of the present town: so it's possible that the name is not derived from St Germanus, but that the proximity of Wales, the familiarity of the saint's name, and Welsh influence in Ireland have led to the recasting of Carman as Garman.

England:

Exeter, Devon: an entry in the *Exeter List of Relics* (11ᵗʰ century) states that relics of St Germanus were in the cathedral there.

Germansweek \ Germanswick, Devon: a church.

Faulkbourne, Essex: a church and holy well.

Winterbourne Farringdon, Dorset: a church.

St Albans, Hertfordshire. Camden, writing towards the end of he 16th Century, states that at St Albans, the site of Germanus' "chapel", above (or beyond) the ruins of the Roman city, yet existed: where the saint preached the divine word from a mound (or platform), as old parchments at St Albans church testified. (For Camden's Latin text, see Chapter 8. For the possible significance of a mound or platform, see See Appendix I, "David and Germanus".)

Thurlby, Scothorne, and *Ranby*, Lincolnshire: three churches grouped about the city of Lincoln.

Wiggenhall St Germans, Norfolk: a church.[2]

Selby, Yorkshire: the Abbey of the Mother of God and St Germanus. In 1068 Benedict, monk of Auxerre, dreamt that St Germanus commanded him to go to England. Obeying him, Benedict brought one of the saint's finger bones to Salisbury, where one Edward made a fine reliquary for it. Benedict was granted another vision which directed him to Selby, where he became a hermit. William the Conqueror granted him land to found a monastery in 1069, which was consecrated in 1070. With time, much land accrued to this institution, and it did not escape dissolution in 1540. The *Historia Selebiensis Monasterii* (1184) records Benedict's experiences, together with miracles and other notable events.

The churches of *Winestead* and *Marske-by-the-Sea*, Yorkshire were consecrated to God in St Germanus' name, probably because they were linked to Selby.

Wirral. T. H. Florence has the following: "The ancient Parish Church [of Wallasey]...is dedicated to St. Hilary of Gaul, a very unusual dedication in this island...St. Germanus taught in Wales when he visited Britain (444 to 450), and it is almost certain that the first wattle Church at Wallasey was dedicated by him or some of his disciples to the Gallican St. Hilary."

And: "There is a local story of a visit of St. Patrick to Bromborough...but this tradition lacks support; although St. Germanus was in Britain in 447 A.D., and they may have arranged to meet."

For these speculations, as for much else of what he has to say concerning the early Church in Britain, the Rev. Florence provides no convincing evidence.

Though St Germanus is not prominent in English ecclesiastical records and calendars, he was recognized. This need not be entirely due to British or Welsh influence, for the Anglo-Saxons and Normans had their own connections with France and Burgundy. Indeed, such was the number of English visitors to Auxerre in mediaeval times that they had their own guesthouse (*xenodocheion*, another Greek term) there.

Continental Europe:

Many French churches are consecrated in the name of a St Germanus, and at least 93 civil communities there bear names beginning "Saint-Germain". However, saints other

168

than the Bishop of Auxerre are also so named: Germanus of Besançon, Germanus of Artois, and Germanus of Paris, for instance. Even so, and bearing in mind that many churches consecrated in memory of St Germanus of Auxerre have not given their names to civil communities (e.g. Mesplède (Pyrénées-Atlantiques), Gazeran et Coignières (Versailles), and Bauneville-sur-Mer (Manche)), it can be seen that such communities as do bear this name are most numerous in three distinct areas. These are east-central France (Burgundy), Brittany and the Normandy \ Lower Seine Valley (including Paris), and the Garonne estuary (see Map 6).

One could expect that Germanus' home area of Burgundy would contain such dedications. Normandy and the Garonne area are not so easily explained: but fugitive (or adventurous) Britons are known to have settled in Normandy as well as Brittany in the 5th and 6th centuries, as dedications there to British saints testify.

They're also known to have ventured beyond the English Channel, and there is evidence of direct links between Britain, the western coast of France and the north coast of Spain during this period. This is especially true of south-west France: for apart from the wealth and wines of Aquitaine itself, the Garonne made for easier and safer passage to the Mediterranean.

Apart from Auxerre, one of the most important churches to bear St Germanus' name is Saint Germain l'Auxerrois in Paris. Directly opposite the Louvre, this was the royal church of France until the court moved to Versailles. Sadly, it was the tolling of this church's bells which

169

announced the beginning of the St Bartholomew's Day Massacre of August the 24th 1572.

The modern Orthodox church at Vézelay is consecrated in the names of St Etienne (Stephen) and Germanus.

Germanus of Auxerre is patron of one of the oldest churches in Geneva, Switzerland. The remains of a 5th-century edifice have been uncovered there.

Locations Connected with Vortigern

Nant Gwrtheyrn, ("Vortigern's Valley") Gwynedd. Here, according to local legend, stood that fortress of Vortigern's which was destroyed by fire: a notable Iron Age hillfort crowns a nearby peak. Also *Bedd Gwrtheyrn* ("Vortigern's Grave"), a cairn wherein he was supposed to have been buried. Thomas Pennant records the opening of this cairn in the 18th century, and that it contained the bones of a tall man. (For this and Dinas Emrys below, see also Chapter 3, note 7).

Dinas Emrys, ("Ambrosius' Fortress") Gwynedd: the site of that fortress of Vortigern's which, according to Nennius, could not be completed until the child Emrys (Ambrosius) discovered the two dragons beneath it.

Caer Gwrtheyrn ("Vortigern's Fortress") on the hill of *Craig Gwrtheyrn* (Vortigern's rock") at Llanfihangel ar Arth, Carmarthenshire, OS Grid Ref. SN 433402. Five hundred yards to the south-west lies *Ffynnon Armon* (or *Iarmon*), "Germanus' Well" (see above).

Little Doward Hill, by Ganarew, Herefordshire. In Chapter 2, Book 8 of Geoffrey of Monmouth's *Historia Regnum Britanniae* (History of the Kings of Britain) it is stated that Vortigern fled from before Ambrosius Aurelianus to "Genoreu" in Wales, in the area of "Hergin" on the banks of the "Gania", where he had a tower on the hill of "Cloartius". This is Little Doward Hill in the parish of Ganarew in the hundred of Erging (Archenfield), on the banks of Wye two miles above Monmouth. There, according to Geoffrey, Ambrosius burnt the tower and all in it, including Vortigern.

Perhaps Geoffrey adapted Nennius' description of Vortigern's fate at Craig Gwrtheyrn in the Teifi Valley for his own audience in the Monmouth region: but it's equally possible that he drew on old Wye Valley traditions. This is supported by sources which describe Vortigern's family as being connected with Archenfield and Gloucester.

Vortigern is named in the *Red Book of Hergest* Triads as one of the "three shameful men", where it is stated that:

"...in the end, Uther and Ambrosius burnt Vortigern, in the Castle of Gwrtheyrnion on the banks of Wye...".

A record likely dervied from Geoffrey of Monmouth: yet Sir J. E. Lloyd suggested that this "castle" may have been at Rhaeadr Gwy (*anglice* Rhayader), and that there may have been a tradition that St Germanus and his accompanying clerics may have stood fasting forty days and nights upon a rock at nearby St Harmons.

Notes

1. Cf. Dolwyddelan, where *Ffynnon yr Offeiriad* (The Priest's Well) and *Sarn yr Offeiriad* (The Priest's Causeway) also occur.

2. Bearing in mind the number of churches consecrated in St Germanus' name in Normandy, the existence of similar churches in eastern England may be connected to William the Conqueror's decision to grant much land to his followers there.

7. Germanus of the Poets

Armes Prydein Vawr

See Appendix 1, "David and Germanus".

Péan Gatineau

In the second quarter of the 13th century the French poet Péan Gatineau sang in praise of St Martin of Tours. He relates how the monks of Tours wandered abroad with Martin's relics, staying awhile in the church of *sainz Germains*: Germanus of Auxerre, perhaps. The faithful visited the church in order to venerate the relics, leaving offerings: but a dispute arose between the local clergy and the monks of Tours regarding how these offerings should be shared between them.

In order to end the dispute, a leper was placed half way between the relics of both saints. One side of his body, that nearest Martin, was healed, with Germanus, according to Gatineau, refraining (for the time being) from healing the other half, out of respect for his saintly visitor. Here are lines 7,845 – 7,852 of the poem in question:

> Et entre les cors sainz poserent
> Un meseau segont lor devise;
> Mes la partie qui fut mise
> Devers saint Martin fut garie
> Tantost de la meselerie,
> Et sainz Germains ot repeitee
> A garir a cele feiee

La part qui fut vers lui posee.

This alleged deferment of St Germanus to St Martin may not be unconnected with rivalry between Tours and Auxerre, as mentioned in Chapter 2.

Welsh Poets of the Late Middle Ages

Welsh poets of the 15th and 16th century also make references to St Germanus in works praising or lamenting their noble patrons, or in praise of the saints. This would be especially apt if St Germanus was connected with the patron's home area or parish.

Lewys Glyn Cothi (c.1425 – c.1489)
From *Gwaith Lewys Glyn Cothi*, ed. Dafydd Johnston, Caerdydd 1995.

i.) To the Saints of Wales (incomplete), ll.44-46.

Dogwel lwyd...	*Holy Dogwel…*
Idloes, Garmon...	*Idloes, Germanus….*
Oswallt wyn...	*Blessèd Oswald…*
Cennych mor...	*Cennych so….*

ii.) In praise of Sir Richard Herbert, ll.5-8.

Nid llai ei dai, deuent – fan fynnon',
Nog yn nhai Armon, nog yn nherment,
Nid llai no'r dengmor na'i dent – na'i drysor,
Nid llai no Winsor na'i stôr na'i stent;

No fewer throng in his halls -come all whenever they
wish –
Than those in Germanus' dwellings, or at a funeral:
No less than the ten seas are his hospitality and wealth;
No less than Windsor, his property and inheritance.

The numbers enjoying Sir Richard's hospitality are no fewer than the worshipers filling St Germanus' churches, or at a well-attended funeral. His generosity marks him out as truly noble and praiseworthy, and the poet hints that this member of a powerful and well-connected family could even be considered worthy of the throne.

iii.) In Praise of William ap Morgan, ll.9-10

Pumwell yw Wiliam i roi pimant,
Myn llaw hen Armon, no holl Normant.

William's five times better than all France
At giving wine, by old Germanus' hand!

Again, the free giving of expensive wine is symptomatic of the patron's inherent nobility. The reference to "old Germanus' hand" could imply comparison with Germanus' generosity, his "open-handedness": or perhaps that that the poet has a specific relic in mind. However, it could be but a general oath, or an alliterative device particularly apt when praising such a magnate as William ap Morgan of Llanarmon yn Iâl. In Simwnt Fychan's ode to King Edward II, for instance, we find:

Y mae'n Lloegr, myn llaw Iago,
Air am ei fraint a'i rym fô.

In England, by [St] James' hand,
There's talk of his privilege and power".

(Roberts, Glyn: *Aspects of Welsh History*, Cardiff 1969, p.264).

iv.) The Lament for Gwenllian, daughter of Owain Glyndŵr, ll.43-48.

> Un ŵyl uchel ni lechynt,
> Na dydd gwaith nac undydd gynt.
> Yr un hwy a roen'ennyd
> Rodd Basg a harddai y byd,
> Rhodd Nadolig is brig bron,
> Rhodd ail ormodd Ŵyl Armon.

> *From no high festival would they refrain,*
> *Nor any workday, nor any day of yore.*
> *Together, they readily gave*
> *An Easter gift that would enrich the world,*
> *A Christmas gift in the lee of the hill,*
> *Likewise an exceptional gift*
> *On Germanus' Feast.*

Again, the everyday generosity of patrons, and especially at Easter, Christmas and the local patronal Feast of St Germanus, underlines their high social standing.

v.) In Praise of Dafydd Goch ap Hywel, ll.1-2, 19-20, 37-38, 47-48.

Dydd da'r gwrola' â'i rôn,
Dewr grymus o dir Garmon...
Mil fry'n amliwiaw y fron,
Teirmil deutu i Armon...
Gan yr hael ef a gâi'n rhodd
O dir Garmon dri gormodd...
Grym dwy wddar, grym deuddeg,
Grym naw o dir Garmon deg.

Greetings to the bravest spear-bearer,
The valiant, mighty one from Germanus' land...
A thousand up there, lending colour to the hillside,
Three thousand, about Germanus' land...
From the generous one, he'd get a gift
From Germanus' land, thrice more than he'd asked...
The strength of two oaks, the strength of twelve [men],
The strength of nine in Germanus' fair land.

Physical strength and valour were other laudable noble virtues. The "land" refers to the parish dedicated in St Germanus' name.

vi.) Asking a Bedspread of Elin, daughter of Llywelyn,
   ll.23-24.

Gormodd, myn eglwys Garmon,
I'm oes yw f'anfoes ar Fôn.

By Germanus' church! My disrespect
Towards Anglesey [folk] was ever extreme.

As St Germanus has no known dedications on Anglesey, this may be an instance of using the saint's name for alliterative effect.

From *The Poetical Works of Lewis Glyn Cothi*, The Honourable Society of Cymmrodorion, Oxford 1837.

The Lament for Rhys and Owain, sons of Phylib ab Rhys of Cenarth, ll.1-4.

Rhys, Owain rymus val yr òn, o bryd
Llaw a braich Sain Harmon,
Aeth y rhain o Wrtheyrnion,
I wlad nev i weled Non.

Rhys and Owain, mighty as spears - In appearance,
Hand and arm of St Harmons,
These departed Gwrtheyrnion,
For the land of Heaven, to see Non.

A lament for two brothers of St Harmons, strong as spears (literally, "ash trees", spear shafts being fashioned from ash wood), as intimately linked with each other as a hand and arm (also symbolizing ability and strength). However, this simile may also refer to reliquaries containing holy hands and arms. Such did exist in Wales, as witnessed by one of silver, in the form of a hand and forearm, found on Bardsey Island in the 19th century (see *Report of the Royal Commission on Ancient and Historical Monuments*, Caernarfonshire, Vol. 3, p.xli).

Interestingly, in discussing the history of the parish of St Harmons, the Rev. Jonathan Williams states:

"Contiguous with Nant-y-Saeson is a single stone

of huge dimensions, placed erect in the earth, and also two large and two small stones arranged quadrangularly, named, called "Dau fraich, a dau law," that is, the two arms and the two hands, near to a place named Hendrew."

Gwyrtheyrnion is the hundred in which St Harmons is situated, and Non would be St Non, mother of St David of Wales (patron saint of the local diocese).

Dafydd Nanmor (before 1450 – c.1490).
From *The Poetical Works of Dafydd Nanmor*, ed. Thomas Roberts, Cardiff 1923.

To Rhys ap Meredudd of Tywyn, ll.39-42.

> I fwrdd tâl a ddyfalwyd
> I allor fawr, lle rhôi fwyd.
> Myn Garmon, digon o dâl
> A bair Duw eb roi dial...

> *His high table, where he gave food,*
> *Was compared to a great altar.*
> *By Germanus! God will reward him well,*
> *And wreak no vengeance [on him]...*

The comparison of the high table to an altar, ablaze with candles, polished vessels and colour, is particularly evocative.

Dafydd ab Edmwnd (before 1450 – c.1497)
From *Gwaith Dafydd ab Edmwnd*, ed. Thomas Roberts, Bangor 1914.

In Praise of Cynfrig and Elin of Lwydiarth, ll.43-46.

> Am roi da nid mwy r dial
> O roddi doir i r ddau dal
> Garmon un gair am yn iaith
> Gair Elin ai gwr eilwaith...

> *For giving gifts and presents,*
> *Both will be rewarded, without penalty.*
> *Germanus' word to our nation,*
> *And again, Elin and her husband's word...*

Tudur Aled (c.1465 – 1526).
From *Gwaith Tudur Aled*, ed. T. Gwyn Jones, Caerdydd 1926.

i.) The Lament for Tudur Llwyd of Bodidris, Iâl, ll.3-4.

> Marw mab mam mawr ym mhob modd,
> Mair a Garmon! Marw gormodd.

> *The death of a mother's son, great in every way,*
> *By Mary and Germanus! Is a death too many.*

ii.) To Tudur Llwyd, ll.59-60.

> Tŵr mawr, o antur a modd,
> Tir Garmon, torr wayw gormodd!

> *Great tower, in venture and means,*
> *Of Germanus' land, breaker of many spears!*

Gutun Owain (before 1460 – c. 1500).

From *L'oeuvre Poétique de Gutun Owain*, ed. E. Bachellery, Paris 1950.

The Lament for Dafydd Llwyd ap Tudur of Bodidris, ll.43-46.

Kalan Ystwyll i'n twyllwyd
Gloi'r bedd ar glera a bwyd.
Gwyl Armon vu'r rroddion rrydd
I ddwyvil tra vu Ddavydd.

On the Eve of Epiphany, we were cheated,
The grave shut upon minstrelsy and food.
On St Germanus' Day, gifts were freely given
To two thousand [people], whilst Dafydd lived.

The above two quotations witness that the local saint's feast was kept with joy, and that the distribution of gifts was part of the celebration.

Saunders Lewis

In 1936, the great Welsh dramatist, poet and patriot Saunders Lewis was commissioned by the BBC to write a radio drama. The result was *Buchedd Garmon* ("The Life of St Germanus"), a *vers libre* rendering of the story of Germanus' visit in 429 AD. Illtud and Paulinus visit Germanus, asking his help against Pelagianism. Germanus and Lupus consent to go, with Germanus defeating the Pelagians in debate, and restoring a blind child's sight. Ambrosius Aurelianus then asks Germanus' help against a Saxon/Pictish army, and the result is the resounding Hallelujah Victory.

181

Though set in the distant past, and portraying the defeat of heresy by the adherents of Augustinism (Lewis was, most unusually for Wales at that time, a staunch Roman Catholic from a Calvinistic Methodist background), the drama was, in reality a call to arms in the defence of the Welsh nation against spiritual and cultural decay, and the onrush of materialism and Anglicization. As Ambrosius ringingly declares:

> My homeland, Wales, is a vineyard given unto my care,
> To be delivered in turn to my children, and unto their children, too,
> An inheritance for all time: and behold, now the swine
> Bear down upon her, furious to ravage and spoil.
> Therefore I now call my friends, learned and unlearned all,
> Come, come and join me in the gap, and stand by my side in the pass,
> That the ages to come may inherit the beauty of yore.

This ground-breaking and influential work was broadcast on the 2nd of March 1937, by which time the author was already in prison for his part in the torching of buildings at the aerial bombing training centre at Penyberth, Pwllheli. It was published by Gwasg Aberystwyth later that year.

8. Gleanings

Gerald of Wales *Descriptio Cambriæ* [The Description of Wales], c. 1191.

Chapter 18: How they received the true religion long ago, their piety and their devotion to the Christian faith.

About two hundred years ago [sic], long before the fall of Britain, the Welsh were instructed and confirmed in the Christian faith by Faganus and Duvianus who, at the request of King Lucius, were sent to the island by Pope Eleutherius. Later on, Germanus of Auxerre and Lupus of Troyes were sent over because of the corruption which had gradually resulted from the invasions of the pagan Saxons, and more especially to put an end to the Pelagian heresy, but they found nothing heretical or contrary to the articles of the true faith. Even today the Welsh still keep up some practices which Germanus and Lupus taught them. When a loaf of bread is put before them, they break off a piece and give it to the poor. They sit down three to a meal in memory of the Holy Trinity. When they meet a monk or priest, or any religious in his habit, they stretch out their arms, bow their heads and ask his blessing. More than any other people they long to be confirmed by a bishop and to receive that mark with the chrism which is the sign of the grace of the Holy Ghost...

When they marry, or go on a pilgrimage, or, on the advice of the clergy, make a special effort to amend their ways, they give a donation of one tenth of all their worldly goods, cattle, sheep and other livestock...they pay greater respect than any other people to their churches, to men in orders, the relics of the saints, bishops' crooks, bells, holy books and the Cross itself...Nowhere can you see hermits and anchorites more abstinent and more spiritually committed than in Wales.

A Verse regarding St Germanus' activities in Britain, from the *St Malo Missal* (1503).

Anglia bis perfidia
Purgavit a Pelagia,
Mitis reddit eloquia,
Verba frangens incendia.

Humphrey Llwyd *Commentarioli Britannicae Descriptionis Fragmentum*, 1572.

Page 57: God's terrible judgement upon the wicked king at Llynclys.

Descripta Gvynedhia ad Povvisiam secundum Cambriæ regnú accedamus, quod tempore Germani Altisidorensis ibidem contra Pelaginam hæresim olim prædicantis, potens fuisse ex eius vita dignoscitur. Cuius Rex ut ibi habetur, quod virum optimum audire recusaverat, occulto & terribili Dei iudicio, cum regina & tota familia in terrae viscera absorptus est, quo in loco non procul ab Osvvaldia est stagnum incognitæ profunditatis Llunclis.i.vorago Palatii in hunc diem dictum. Multæque ecclesiæ per illam provinciam nomini Germani dictatæ inveniuntur.

Lucy Toulmin Smith *The Itinerary in Wales of John Leland in or about the years 1536-39*. London 1906.

Page 70:

Yale lordship yoinith to Bromefeld upon the farther side of De Ryver, and there is no parte of it on the hither side of Dee. There is in it a 4. or 5. paroches, wherof the moste famose is Llanarmon, *i.e.* Fanum Germani, and Llan Tegla, *i.e.* Fanum Teclae.

Greate pilgremage and offering was a late to S. Armon.

William Camden *Britannia; sive Florentissimorum Regnorum, Angliae, Scotiae, Hiberniae et Insularum Adiacentum ex intima antiquitate Chronographica dessriptio...*Francofurdi [Frankfurt] 1590.

Page 315: St Albans.

...Germanum Antisiodorensum, & Lupum Tricassinum e Gallia euocarent, qui refutata haeresi se venerabiles Britannis reddiderunt, inprimus Germanus, qui plurima per hanc insulam templa sibi sacrata habet, & in ipsa huius prostratis urbis area, Germani sacellum etiamnum super est, quo loci ille pro suggestu verbum divinum effatus erat, ut antiquae fane Albani membranulae testatur.

Sacellum may be translated as a small monumental chapel, funerary chapel, unroofed enclosure with an altar, or small roofless shrine. This may indicate that the place in question was a roofless ruin. *Pro suggero* translates as "[preaching] from an artificial mound, platform, stage or tribune".

B. M. Lansdowne III: the secret testimony of a government agent regarding Welsh political and religious disloyalty to the current regime, c.1600-1610. Judging by the saints named (including "Jermō", Germanus), Ifor Williams suggested that the following was witnessed in the Arfon area of north-west Wales.

"Upon the Sondaies and hollidaies the multitude of all sortes of men women and childerne of everie parishe do use to meete in sondrie places either one some hill or on the side of some mountaine where theire harpers and crowthers singe them songs of the doeings of theire auncestors, namelie, of theire warrs againste the kings of this realme and the English nacion, and then doe they rip upp their petigres at length how eche of them is discended from those theire ould primcs. Here alsoe doe they spende theire time in hearinge some part of the lives of Thalaassyn, Marlin Beno Kybbye Jermō, and suche other the intended propetts and saincts of that cuntrie".

This paragraph is quoted by Sir Ifor Williams in 'Hen Chwedlau.' Trans. Cymm. 1946-47, page 28 of MS B. M. Lansdowne III, f. 110 as found in *A Catalogue of the Manuscripts Relating to Wales in the British Museum*, 1. 72: but better readings are suggested in footnote 2, and are herein incorporated.

Archbishop James Ussher *Britanicorum Ecclesiarum Antiquitates* (1639).

In anonymo de Ecclesiastoricum Officiorum origine, 900. abhinc annis scripto libello, Germanun & Lupum

186

Ordinem cursus Gallorum (sive Gallicanam liturgam) à Iohanne Cassiano & Lirinensis cœnobii patribus acceptum, in Britanniam induxisse legimus. "Beatissimus Cassianus" (inquit author) "qui Linerensi monasterio beatum Honoratum habuit corporem, et post ipsum beatus Honoratus primus Abba, et sanctus Cæsarius episcopus qui fuit in Arelate, et beatus Porcarius Abba qui in ipso Monasterio fuit, ipsum Cursum decantaverunt. Qui beatum Lupum et beatum Germanum monachos in eorum monasterio habuerunt: et ipsi sub normam regulæ ipsum cursum ibidem decantaverunt. Et posteà in Episcopatus cathedra summi honoris (pro reverentiâ sanctitatis eorum) sunt adepti: et posteà in Britaniis vel Scotiis prædicaverunt quæ Vita beati Germani episcopi Antisidorensis et Vita beati Lupi adfirmat.

MS in Bibliothecâ Cottonianâ.

Discourse on the Religion Anciently Professed by the Irish and British (Dublin, 1815.)

Quoting form the works of Dr James Ussher, 1639:

Page 31:

As for the form of the liturgy, or public service of God, which St. Patrick brought into this country: it is said he received it from Germanus and Lupus; and that it originally descended from St. Mark the Evangelist. For so I have seen it set down in an ancient fragment, written well nigh 900 years since, remaining now in the library of Sir Robert Coton, my worthy friend...

In the book of Landaffe...we read that Germanus and Lupus did consecrate chief doctor over all the Britons inhabiting the right* side of Brittany, St. Dubricius....

*By *dextralis partis Britanniae*, it's likely that the southern part of Britain is meant.

Edward Lhuyd *Parochialia*, c.1699.

Archaeologia Cambrensis, April 1909 supplement (The First Part).

Page 22, Llanrwst.

Y Mynydhoedh

1.Darn o Vynydh hiraethog
2.Mynydd gâllt y Kelyn yng Garth Garmon &c.

April 1910 supplement (The Second Part).

Page 14: Achae Seint Ynys Brydain ["Bonedd y Saint"]. Kinmel MS Vol.3 folio 82 onward.

Garmon ap Ridicus ac yn oes Gwrtheyrn Gwrtheneu y doeth i'r Ynys hon ac o Frainc yr hanoedd B.
(Germanus son of Ridicus and in the days of Vortigern he came to this Isle and he hailed from France)

Garmawn m. Ridicus ac en oes Gortheyrn Gortheneu e doeth er enys...

188

B = Lib Joh[S] Brook (Llyvr Jo. Brook o Vowdhwy) pen[es] Dominum Johannem Parry Rect. Eccles. S[ti] Georgii in Com. Denb.

[According to a late version of the Life of St Germanus, his father was named "Rusticus". This assertion found its way into the mediaeval Welsh *Bonedd y Saint* (Genealogy of the Saints), and was afterwards elaborated by writers such as Edward Williams (Iolo Morgannwg). Following his lead, Rice Rees, John Jones and the Rev. W. R. Ambrose further elaborated the tale to the effect that Rusticus was identified with St Cred(f)yw (alias Rhedyw) of Llanllyfni. It was also stated that Cred(f)yw had held an important position in the Church at Autun, and was also the grandfather of Emyr Llydaw: a most questionable claim, given the chronology. In truth, the entire body of Williams' pronouncements concerning St Germanus, "Garmon ap Rhedyw", "Garmon ap Rhedig" and "Garmon ap Goronwy of Gwaredog" can be dismissed as products of his most fertile imagination. Earlier (16th- and 17th-Century) manuscripts state that Cred(f)yw was Emyr Llydaw's great-grandson, and make no mention of Germanus in that context.]

July 1909 supplement (The Third Part).

E. Lhuyd's Notes, October the 16th 1671.

Page 109: Llanarmon in Yale…

Page 112: On the south wall without the s[d] church is affixed the statue of S. German al's Garmon standing, his

189

head, shoulders & armes & feet bare with armes & hands laid flat palmes inwards but erected upon his breast & his girdle downe to his Ankles wrapt about with severall folds of cloaths.

Page 113: (Capel Garmon)

Mem Dr. Coket gathering vipers (snakes) in Ghwn Annog in Garth Garmon.

Archaeologia Cambrensis Series 3, No.6 (1860), p.237 Robert Williams of Rhydycroesau (Oswestry)'s copy of the corresponent "G. R."'s letter to Edward Lhuyd.

Responsa G. R. ad Quæstiones D^{mi} E. Lh.

Moles illae lapidum quæ summitates montium tenet, ideo aggeratae dicuntur, ut sint virorum qui antiquis Britonum bellis succuberunt monumenta, et posteris in memoriam signa ad eundem fere nunc temporis modum qui sibi mortem consciscunt in triviis humantur. Ubi a filiis Edwal Voel & Howel Dha sanguineo praelio dimicatum est, non paucae extant lapidum moles, quae inserviunt pro caesorum monumentis, nec procul abhinc distat Carnedh Owen & Run; hic etiam est bron & Bedh Alarch, cuius patris Lhowarch benedictio ironica frequens volitat per ora virum. Huic loco finitima sunt Germani rostra vulgo vocata Pall Garmon. (Palh Thronus Dav. Lexic.).....

Peris quosdam ex suis Torgochiaid Germano (cuius nomen in Bettws Garmon:) hic autem pauculos ex illis quos dono acceperat S^{cto} Grediw dedit; quorum alter acceptos in Lhyn Cwellyn, alter in stagno Llyn cwm y Dulyn vicino, Llyn Torgochiad inde vocato, ad multiplicandum posuit. Germani Torgochiad sunt illis minores et his majores tan numero tam magnitudine, secundum quæ tempus ad eos successive captandos continuatur. Non ego solus credo hos pisces nullum, aquâ exeptâ, alimentum habere. (Probatum est)

As translated by Dr Bruce Griffiths of Bangor:

"It's said that those cairns of stones upon the mountain tops were piled up for this purpose, that they are in memory of the men who fell in the ancient wars of the Britons, and as reminders to their successors, in the same manner as suicides are these days buried at crossroads. Where there was bloody battle between the sons of Idwal and Hywel the Good, there yet remain not a few cairns, which serve as memorials to the slain, and not far from here stand the Cairns of Owain and Rhun; here also are Alarch's Slope and Grave, whose father Llywarch's ironic benediction is yet heard in the mouths of men. By this place stands Germanus' [platform/pulpit/throne] colloquially named Pall Garmon (Palh Thronus in Davies' Dictionary [*Dictionarum Duplex*, John Davies of Mallwyd, 1632]) ...

Peris [gave] some of his *torgochiaid* to Germanus (his name in Betws Garmon); he [in turn] gave

191

some of the smaller ones he'd received as a gift to Saint Gredyw, of which one [St Germanus] placed those he'd received in Llyn Cwellyn, and the other [St Gredyw] placed some in nearby Llyn Cwm y Dulyn, consequently called "Llyn Torgochiaid", so that they would multiply. Germanus' *torgochiaid* are smaller than those, and larger than these, in both number and size, according to how long the season for catching them lasts [*meaning here very obscure*]. It's not I alone who believes that they have no food other than water. (Proven)"

Until recently, this fish (Arctic Char, *Salvelinus alpinus*) was present in the lakes of Llyn Peris, Llyn Padarn, Llyn Cwellyn and Llyn Bodlyn in Gwynedd, north-west Wales. There is verbal testimony to the effect that they were present in Llyn Dulyn until about 1900, and that Nantlle quarrymen used to angle for them in that lake. However, Mr Walter Hanks of Environment Agency Wales informs the present writer that "the old people still maintain that *torgochiaid* remain in Llyn Dulyn". Interestingly, in the light of "G.R."'s statement, Mr Hanks also tells me that Llyn Cwellyn *torgochiaid* are smaller than those in Llyn Padarn.

According to the *Torgoch Questionnaire* published in the North Wales Gazette in 1809, the *torgoch* fishing season at Llyn Padarn and Llyn Peris then lasted from November to the end of December. The Llyn Cwellyn season was the month of January. It was believed at the time that *torgochiaid* could migrate underground between these lakes, in order to avoid the angling. There are no variations in the *torgoch* fishing season today.

Due to the Dinorwig hydro-electric scheme, *torgochiaid* from Llyn Peris were removed to Ffynnon Llugwy in the Ogwen catchment, and Llyn Eigiau in the Conwy catchment. From Llyn Eigiau they've migrated to Llyn Cowlyd and Llyn Coety. An attempt was made to introduce them into Llynnoedd Diwaunedd on the slopes of Moel Siabod (Conwy catchment), but they didn't thrive there.

The place in which "G. R." wrote his comments isn't known, but he's referring to Snowdonia. From what he wrote, we may be certain that *Pall Garmon* was in the Llanrwst \ Capel Garmon area. *Pall* is an obscure Welsh noun, which could mean "mantle", "platform", "throne" or "house". The Rev. Ellis Davies translates it as "pulpit". In Bodleian Rawlinson MS B.464 fol.9 (Edward Lhuyd's *Parochialia*), the following note is found:

> "Y palh oedh gynt wrth Gappel Garmon. Mem. Gerrig ar i penne yn y dhaiar mewn lhe a elwir Ogo y Ty'n y Koed."

> *"The 'pall' was formerly by Capel Garmon. Mem. Stones stood on end in the earth at a place called Ty'n y Coed Cave".*

On page 323 of the Rev. Ellis Davies' *Prehistoric and Roman Remains of Denbighshire*, we find:

> "CHAMBERED LONG CAIRN – "CROMLECH": CAPEL GARMON. SITE. This monument, locally known as "Yr Ogof", (The Cave) and "Y Gromlech," is situated about ¾ m. To the S.E. of

Capel Garmon Church. The field...bears the name of Cae'r Ogof, and belongs to the farm of Tyn-y-coed."

We may safely state, therefore, that *Pall Garmon* is none other than the Neolithic buial chamber at Capel Garmon.

The Maes Garmon Obelisk Inscription.

Pennant, Thomas. A Tour in Wales, Vol. 1, p.409. London: 1778

Ad Annum
CCCCXX
Saxones Pictiq. Bellum adversus
Britones junctis viribus susciperunt
In hac regione Hodieq. MAESGARMON
appellata; cum in prælium descenditur,
Apostolicis *Britonum* Ducibus Germano
et LUPO, CHRISTUS militabat in Castris:
ALLELUIA tertio repetitum exclamabant
Hostile agmen terrore prosternitur:
Triumphant
Hostibus fusis sine sanguine
palma Fide, non Viribus obtenta
M. P.
in VICTORIÆ ALLELUIATICÆ memoriam
N. G.
MDCCXXXVI.

Cloch Armon (St Germanus' Bell).

Canon Fisher, *The Welsh Celtic Bells.* *Archaeologia Cambrensis* Vol LXXXI (1926), pp.324-334.

194

"There are six of these bells known still to exist in Wales...found thus according to their original parishes...St Garmon's, at Llanarmon...

St. Garmon's bell is of cast bronze, with an iron clapper; height to handle 5½ in., including handle 6¾ in., and 4½ in. by 4 in. across at its mouth. The handle has two loops for the fingers. It is in good condition, and is kept in the parish chest in the vestry at Llanarmon. The late rector of the parish, the Rev. John Davies, B.A., informs me that it was used once during his incumbency, at the funeral of Dr. Walter Ebner Williams, of Portmadoc, on June 30, 1911, at the request of the deceased, who was an antiquary. The rector, with the clerk and surpliced choir, met the body at the churchyard gate, and carrying the bell in his hand, tolled it as they proceeded."

The Llanarmon in question is that in Eifionydd, Gwynedd. Canon Fisher's article includes a photograph of this and other, similar handbells.

Dafydd Pritchard's recollections concerning Betws Garmon. Manuscript, 1964.

Sefydlwyd y Betws yma gan Sant Germanus yn amser rhyfeloedd y Groes neu fel y galwai'r Sais hi, The Crusade War. Dwed traddodiad mai i fyny ar ochr Hafod y Wern roedd yr hen Fetws. Amcan sefydlu y Betws yma oedd er mwyn cael lle i orphwys, ac i gael ymgeledd ar ei taith wrth gludo corph rhyw sant neu gilydd i'w gladdu yn Enlli. Ac yna wrth ddod yn ol i weddio dros ei enaid oedd yn y purdan am rhyw amser nai gilydd. Nid oes ar gael hyd y gwn i, ddim o gofnodion beth oedd yn cael ei gario ymlaen yma na phwy oedd yn gofalu am y lle.

Garmon as a personal name.

Wade-Evans (1950) claimed that the name "Garbaniaun" which appears in Pedigree X of Harleian MS. 3859 is to be interpreted as "Germinianus", and testifies to Germanus' political influence in Strathclyde. However, it could as well be derived from the Irish name "Garban/Gabran", with a territorial suffix, as in the case of Gwrtheyrn/Gwrtheyrnion.

"Garmon" as a forename is very rarely found before the mid-20th century, but gained popularity following the broadcast and publication of Saunders Lewis' *Buchedd Garmon*. However, a "David ap Jerman Rees" was named among those suspected of murdering Henry de Shaldeford near Bangor in 1345. (Roberts, Glyn: Aspects of Welsh History, Cardiff 1969, p.194.) T. E. Morris had it that the surname "Harman" in Herefordshire derives from "Garmon": but according to the National Trust's map of surname distributions in 1881, the occurrence of "Harman" is strongly concentrated in south-east England, and barely, if at all, on the Welsh borders.

Troparion to St Germanus of Auxerre, sung by the Orthodox of France.

Saint évêque Germain, notre protecteur, honneur et consolation de l'Église de Gaule.
Tu as quitté la gloire et les richesses pour suivre avec humilité le Christ notre Dieu.
Tu as combattu les hérésies et fait triompher la vraie Foi.

196

Ô père des Auxerrois, refuge des malheureux, prie de Christ de nous affermir dans Sa miséricorde.

Bibliography

Here is a catalogue of the sources of this work.

Ab Ithel, J. W. "Moel Fenlli". *Cambrian Journal*, i (1854).

Ab Owain, S. *Hynodion Gwlad y Bryniau*. Llanrwst: Gwasg Carreg Gwalch, 2000.

Ambrose, W. R. *Hynafiaethau, Cofiannau a Hanes Presennol Nant Nantlle*. Pen-y-groes: Griffith Lewis, 1872.

Anon. "Saint John of Colonia." In: *The Holy Martyr Longinus the Centurion*. Lives of the Saints, 15. Sydney: Orthodox Monastery of the Archangel Michael, 1997.

_____. *Montgomery Collections* ii (1869), xlix (1946)

Bachellery, E. (ed.). *L'oeuvre Poétique de Gutun Owain*. Paris: Librairie Ancienne Honoré Champion, 1950.

Bălan, Archimandrite Ioanichie. *Romanian Patericon*, Vol. 1. Platina: St Herman of Alaska Brotherhood, 2005.

Baring-Gould, S., a Fisher, J. *Lives of the British Saints* (8 vols). Felinfach: Llanerch Publishers, 2000.

Bartrum, P. C. *A Welsh Classical Dictionary*. Aberystwyth: National Library of Wales, 1993.

Bede. *Ecclesiastical History of the English People*. London: Penguin Books, 1990.

Bell, H. I. *Vita Sancti Tathei and Buchedd Seint y Katrin*. Bangor: The Bangor Welsh Manuscripts Society, 1909.

Bowen, E. G. *Saints, Seaways and Settlements in the Celtic Lands*. Cardiff: University of Wales Press, 1977.

Breeze, A. "St Patrick's Birthplace." *The Welsh Journal of Religious History*, Vol. 3 (2008).

Bromwich, R. "The Character of Early Welsh Tradition." In: Chadwick, H. M. *et al. Studies in Early British History.* Cambridge: University Press, 1954.

Brown, P. "Pelagius and his Supporters: Aims and Environment." *Journal of Theological Studies* XIX (1968).

Cartwright, J. (ed.). *Celtic Hagiography and Saints' Cults.* Cardiff: University of Wales Press, 2003.

Chadwick, N. K. "St. Ninian." In: *Dumfreisshire and Galloway Natural History and Antiquarian Society. Transactions and Journal of Proceedings* 1948-49. Third Series, Vol. XXVII, pp.47-48. Dumfries, 1950.

_____. "A Note on the Name Vortigern." In: Chadwick, H. M. *et al. Studies in Early British History.* Cambridge: University Press, 1954.

_____. "A Note on Faustus and Riocatus." In: Chadwick, H. M. *et al. Studies in Early British History.* Cambridge: University Press, 1954.

_____. "Early Culture and Learning in North Wales." In: Chadwick, N. K. *et al. Studies in the Early British Church.* Cambridge: University Press, 1958.

Chrysostomos of Etna, Archbishop. "Orthodoxy and the Cults." In: *Contemporary Traditionalist Orthodox Thought.* Etna: Center for Traditionalist Orthodox Studies, 1986.

Cooper-Marsdin, A. C. *The History of the Islands of the Lerins.* Cambridge: Cambridge University Press, 1913.

Cymdeithas Ffynhonnau Cymru. *Llygad y Ffynnon,* 19 (Nadolig 2005).

Cymmrodorion Record Series, No.6: *The Episcopal Registers of the Diocese of St. Davids 1397 to 1518.* London 1917.

D'Achéry, L., and Mabillon, J. *Acta Sanctorum Ordinis S. Benedicti*, Vol. 1. Venice: Coleti & Bettinelli, 1733.

Damascene, Hieromonk. "The Place of Saints in the Spiritual Life." *Orthodox Word* 221 (November-December 2001).

_____. *Father Seraphim Rose: his Life and Works*. Platina: St Herman of Alaska Brotherhood, 2005.

_____. "Created in Incorruption: The Orthodox Patristic Understanding of Man and the Cosmos in Their Original, Fallen and Redeemed States." *The Orthodox Word* 258-259 (January-April 2008).

Dark, K. *Britain and the End of the Roman Empire*. Stroud: Tempus Publishing Ltd, 2000.

Davies, The Rev. Ellis. *The Prehistoric & Roman Remains of Denbighshire*. Cardiff: The Author, 1929.

Davies, Aubrey. "Llanbeblig Parish Church." *Caernarvonshire Historical Society Transactions* 20 (1959).

Davies, E. T. *An Ecclesiastical History of Monmouthshire*, Part 1. Risca: Starsons (Publishers) Ltd, 1953.

Davies, John. *Hanes Cymru*. London: Allen Lane (Penguin), 1990.

Davies, J. B. *The Saints of Wales*. Catholic Truth Society (Welsh Province), 1969.

Davies, W., and Jones, J. (eds). *The Poetical Works of Lewis Glyn Cothi*. Oxford: The Honourable Society of Cymmrodorion, 1837.

Davies, Wendy. "The Myth of the Celtic Church." In: Edwards, N, and Lane, A (eds.): *The Early Church in Wales and the West*. Oxbow Monograph 16. Oxford: Oxbow Books, 1992.

Doble, G. H. *Saint Iltut*. Cardiff: University of Wales Press Board, 1944.

Duffy, E. *The Stripping of the Altars*. Newhaven: Yale University Press, 2005.

Dumville, D. N. "Late Seventh- or Eighth-Century Evidence for the British Transmission of Pelagius." *Cambridge Medieval Celtic Studies* 10 (Winter 1985), 39-52.

Edwards, O. T. "The Office of St David in Paris, Bibliothèque Nationale, MS lat. 17294." In: Evans, J. W., and Wooding, J. M. (eds.) *St David of Wales: Cult, Church and Nation*. Woodbridge: Boydell Press, 2007.

Ellis, T. P. *Yr Eglwys Catholig yng Nghymru dan yr Ymerodraeth Rfain* [sic]. London: Catholic Truth Society, 1931.

Evans, E. "Original Documents." *Cylchgrawn Llyfrgell Genedlaethol Cymru* VI (1949-50).

Evans, H. C., and Wixon, W.D. (eds). *The Glory of Byzantium*. New York: Metropolitan Museum of Art, 1997.

Evans, R. F. *Pelagius: Inquiries and Appraisals*. New York: The Seabury Press, 1968.

Ewig, E. "Bemerkungen zur Vita des Bischofs Lupus von Troyes." In: Hauck, K, and Mordek, H. (eds). *Geschichtsschreibung und Geistiges heben im Mittelalter*. Köln: Böhlau Verlag, 1978.

Farmer, D. H. *The Oxford Dictionary of Saints*. Oxford: Clarendon Press, 1978.

Faulkner, N., and Neal, D. "The end of Roman Verulamium." In: *Current Archaeology* 237 (December 2009), pp. 29-35.

Fenn, R. W. D. "The Age of the Saints." In: Walker, D. (ed.). *A History of the Church in Wales*. Penarth: Church in Wales Publications, 1990.

201

Fisher, Canon. "The Welsh Celtic Bells." *Archaeologia Cambrensis* LXXXI (1927).

Florence, The Revd. T. H. *Notes on the History of the Early British (Celtic) Church 1 – 680 A.D*. Birkenhead: The Author, 1961.

Frazer, Sir J. *The Golden Bough*. London: Wordsworth Editions Ltd., 1993.

Gardner, W. "The Ancient hill Fort on Moel Fenlli, Denbighshire." *Archaeologia Cambrensis* LXXVI (1921), pp. 249 – 257.

George, Archimandrite. *The Lord's Prayer*. Gregoriou Monastery, Mount Athos, 1997.

Gibson, E. C. S. "John Cassian." In: Schaff, P., and Wace, H. (eds.). *A Select Library of Nicene and Post-Nicene Fathers of the Christian Church*. Second Series: Volume XI. Grand Rapids: Wm. B. Eerdmans, 1982.

Goddard, H. O. "Aenach Carman: Its Site." In: *Journal of the Royal Society of Antiquaries of Ireland*, Vol. 36, No. 1 (1906), pp. 11-12.

Greenhalgh, P., and Eliopoulos, E. *Deep Into Mani*. London: Faber & Faber, 1985.

Gruffydd, Eirlys. *Ffynhonnau Cymru* (Volume 1). Llanrwst: Gwasg Carreg Gwalch, 1997.

Gruffydd, Eirlys a Ken Lloyd. *Ffynhonnau Cymru* (Volume 2). Llanrwst: Gwasg Carreg Gwalch, 1999.

"H.H." *Eglwysi Llangybi a Llanarmon*. Llanystundwy: Eglwys Llanystumdwy, nd.

Henderson, Charles. "The Ecclesiastical Antiquities of the 109 Parishes of West Cornwall." *Journal of the Royal Institution of Cornwall*, Volume III, Part 2, 1958.

Henig, M. "Religion and Art in St Alban's City." In: Henig, M., and Lindley, P. *Alban and St Albans.* Leeds: British Archaeological Association, Conference Transactions XXIV, 2001.

Heurtley, C. A. "Vincent of Lérins." In: Schaff, P., and Wace, H. (eds.). *A Select Library of Nicene and Post-Nicene Fathers of the Christian Church.* Second Series: Volume XI. Grand Rapids: Wm. B. Eerdmans, 1982.

Hoare, F. R., (ed). *The Western Fathers.* New York: Harper Torchbooks, 1954.

Howlett, D. "Literate Culture of 'Dark Age' Britain." *British Archeology* 33, April 1998.

Hunt, Tony. *Oxford Journals: French Studies* 58, No. 3, July 2004.

Huws, J. O. *Straeon Gwerin Ardal Eryri.* Vol. 2. Llanrwst: Gwasg Carreg Gwalch, 2008.

Hylson-Smith, K. *Christianity in England from Roman Times to the Reformation.* London: SCM Press, 1999.

James, J. W. *Rhigyfarch's Life of St. David.* Cardiff: University of Wales Press, 1967.

Jarman, A. O. H. *Llyfr Du Caerfyrddin.* Caerdydd: Gwasg Prifysgol Cymru,1982.

Jenner, H. "The Lannaled Mass of St. Germans in Bodl. MS." *Journal of the Royal Institution of Cornwall,* XXIII, Parts 3 and 4, 1931-32.

Isaac, G. R. "Armes Prydain Fawr and St David." In: Evans, J. W., and Wooding, J. M. (eds.) *St David of Wales: Cult, Church and Nation.* Woodbridge: Boydell Press, 2007.

John, T., a Rees, N. *Pilgrimage: A Welsh Perspective.* Llandysul: Gwasg Gomer, 2002.

Johnson, Dafydd (ed.). *Gwaith Lewys Glyn Cothi*.
    Caerdydd: Gwasg Prifysgol Cymru,1995.
Johnson, Stephen. *Later Roman Britain*. London: Book Club
    Associates, 1980.
Jones, A. *The History of Gruffydd ap Cynan*. Manchester:
    Manchester University, 1910.
Jones, E. J. *History of Education in Wales* (Volume 1).
    Wrexham: Hughes & Son, 1931.
Jones, Francis. *The Holy Wells of Wales*. Cardiff: University
    of Wales Press, 1992.
Jones, John. "Segontiaci." *Archaeologia Cambrensis* 2 (1847).
Jones, Owen; Williams, Edward; and Owen, William. *The
    Myvyrian Archaiology of Wales*, Vol. 1. London: The
    Editors, 1801.
Jones, M. E. "The Historicity of the Alleluja Victory."
    Albion 18 (1986).
_____. "Saint Germanus and the Adventus Saxonum."
    Haskins Society Journal 2 (1990).
Jones, T. *Gerallt Gymro*. Caerdydd: Gwasg Prifysgol
    Cymru, 1938.
_____. *Brut y Tywysogion*. Caerdydd: Gwasg Prifysgol
    Cymru, 1941.
Jones, T. Gwyn (ed.). *Gwaith Tudur Aled*. Caerdydd:
    Gwasg Prifysgol Cymru, 1926.
Kinvig, R. H. *The Isle of Man*. Liverpool: Liverpool
    University Press, 1975.
Kirby, D. P. "Vortigern." *Bulletin of the Board of Celtic
    Studies* XXIII, Part I (November 1968).
_____. "British Dynastic History in the Pre-Viking
    Period." *Bulletin of the Board of Celtic Studies* XXVII,
    Part I (November 1976).
Knight, J. K. *The End of Antiquity*. Stroud: Tempus
    Publishing, 2007.

Krusch, B. and Levison, W. (eds) "Vita Lupi." In: *Passiones vitaeque sanctorum aevi merovingici et antiquiorum aliquot*, VII. Hannover, 1919-1920.

Lack, K. *The Eagle and the Dove*. London: Triangle, 2000.

Lake, K. (transl.) "The Shepherd of Hermas." In: Page, T. E., and Rouse, W. H. D. (eds). *The Apostolic Fathers*, Volume II. London: William Heinemann, 1913.

Lapidge, M. "Gildas's Education." In: Lapidge, M., and Dumville, D. (eds). *Gildas: New Approaches*. Woodbridge: The Boydell Press, 1984.

Lewis, E. A. "Select Montgomeryshire Deeds: Henry VIII to Elizabeth." *Montgomery Collections* XLIX (1946).

Lewis, Saunders. *Buchedd Garmon*. Aberystwyth: Gwasg Aberystwyth, 1937.

Lhuyd, E. "Parochialia." Part I. *Archaeologia Cambrensis*, Appendix April 190

_____. Part II. *Archaeologia Cambrensis*, Appendix April 1910.

_____. Part III. *Archaeologia Cambrensis*, Appendix July 1911.

Lhuyd, H. *Commentarioli Britannicae Descriptionis Fragmentum*. Köln, 1572.

Lloyd, The Chevalier J. Y. W. "History of the Lordship of Maelor Gymraeg or Bromfield..." *Archaeologia Cambrensis* 1872, p. 283.

_____. *The History of the Princes, and Lords Marcher, and The Ancient Nobility of Powys Fadog*, Volume 2. London: T. Richards, 1881-87.

Lloyd, Sir J. E. *A History of Wales from the Earliest times to the Edwardian Conquest*. London: Longmans, Green & Co., 1954.

Macaulay, Rose. *The Towers of Trebizond*. London: Collins, 1956.

Markus, R. A. "Pelagianism: Britain and the Continent." *Journal of Ecclesiastical History* 37 (1986).

Mathisen, R. W. "The Last Year of Saint Germanus of Auxerre." *Analecta Bollandina* 99 (1981).

Moore, A. W. *A History of the Isle of Man*. London, 1900.

Morris, J. "Pelagian Literature." *Journal of Theological Studies* (new series) 16 (1965).

_____. "The Dates of the Celtic Saints." *Journal of Theological Studies* (new series) 17 (1966).

_____. *The Age of Arthur*. London: Phillimore & Co., 1977.

Morris, T. E. "Welsh Surnames in the Border Counties of Wales." *Y Cymmrodor*, 43 (1932), p. 106 and table p. 173.

Myres, J. N. L. "Pelagius and the End of Roman Rule in Britain." *Journal of Roman Studies* 50 (1960).

Nankivell, Father J. "Bede's World: Early Christianity in the British Isles." *Road to Emmaus* Volume 8 No. 3 (#30) (Summer 2007).

Niblett, R. "Why Verulamium?" In: Henig, M. and Lindley, P. *Alban and St Albans*. Leeds: *British Archaeological Association Conference Transactions* XXIV, 2001.

O'Loughlin, T. *Discovering Saint Patrick*. London: Darton, Longman & Todd, 2005.

Orme, Nicholas. *The Saints of Cornwall*. Oxford: Oxford University Press, 2000.

Owen, Elias. "Wednesday, August 23rd. Excursion No 2." *Archaeologia Cambrensis* 1894, p.147.

Owen, George (ed. H. Owen): *The Description of Pembrokeshire*. London 1892.

Pennant, Thomas. *A Tour in Wales*. Downing: The Author, 1778 and 1781.

Petts, David. *Christianity in Roman Britain*. Stroud: Tempus, 2003.

Pritchard, T. W. *The Parish Church of St. Garmon, Llanarmon yn Iâl, Clwyd*. nd.

Rees, Rice. *An Essay on Welsh Saints*. London: Longman, Rees, Orme, Brown, Green and Longman, 1836.

Rees, William. *An Historical Atlas of Wales from Early to Modern Times*. London: Faber and Faber, 1968.

Radford, C. A. R. "The Church of St. Germans." *Journal of the Royal Institution of Cornwall*, New Series VII, Part 3, 1975/6.

Richards, Gwynfryn. "Llanllyfni: An Unusual Dedication." *Transactions of the Caernarvonshire Historical Society* 28 (1967).

Richards, Melville. "Nennius's 'Regio Guunnessi'." *Transactions of the Caernarvonshire Historical Society* 24 (1963).

Richards, T. *A Slight Historical and Topographical Sketch of the Parish of Llanfechain in the County of Montgomery*. London: T. Richards 1872.

Roberts, A. "Sulpitius Severus." In: Schaff, P., and Wace, H. (eds.). *A Select Library of Nicene and Post-Nicene Fathers of the Christian Church*. Second Series: Volume XI. Grand Rapids: Wm. B. Eerdmans, 1982.

Roberts, Glyn. *Aspects of Welsh History*. Cardiff: University of Wales Press, 1969.

Roberts, Thomas (ed.). *Gwaith Dafydd ab Edmwnd*. Bangor: Bangor Welsh Manuscripts Society, 1914

Roberts, Thomas (ed.). *The Poetical Works of Dafydd Nanmor*. Cardiff: University of Wales Press, 1923.

Rose, Father Seraphim. "The Place of Blessed Augustine in the Orthodox Church." *Orthodox Word* 79 (March/April 1978) and 80 (May/June 1978).

Rowley, R. *Historia Britonum.* Cribin: Llanerch Press, 2005.

Report of the Royal Commission on Ancient and Historical Monuments. Inventory of Ancient Monuments of Wales. Caernarvonshire (Central). London: HMSO, (1960)

_____. Caernarvonshire (West) (1964)

Report of the Royal Commission on Ancient and Historical Monuments. Inventory of Ancient Monuments of Wales and Monmouthshire. Carmarthenshire. London: HMSO, (1917).

_____. Denbighshire (1914)

_____. Flintshire (1912)

_____. Montgomeryshire i. (1911)

_____. Pembrokeshire (1925)

_____. Radnorshire (1913)

Russell, M. "Rewriting the Age of Arthur." *Current Archaeology* 229 (Vol. XX, No. 1), April 2009.

Rutt, The V. Rev. R. "Missa Propria Germani and the Eponym of St. Germans." *Journal of the Royal Institution of Cornwall,* New Series VII, Part 4, 1977.

Sharpe, R. "The late antique Passion of St Alban." In: Henig, M., and Lindley, P. *Alban and St Albans.* Leeds: *British Archaeological Association Conference Transactions* XXIV, 2001.

Sharpe, R., and Davies, J. R. "Rhygyfarch's Life of St David." In: Evans, J. W., and Wooding, J. M. (eds.) *St David of Wales: Cult, Church and Nation.* Woodbridge: Boydell Press, 2007.

Smith, L. T. *The Itinerary in Wales of John Leland in or about the years 1536-39.* London, 1906.

Snyder, C. A. *An Age of Tyrants*. Stroud: Sutton
    Publishing, 1998.

"T". "Miscellaneous note." *Archaeologia Cambrensis 1884*,
    p. 146.

Taylor, H. O. *The Emergence of Christian Culture in the West*.
    New York: Harper and Brothers, 1958.

Thomas, A. M. *Cyffesion Awstin Sant*. Caernarfon: Llyfrfa'r
    M.C., 1973.

Thomas, C. *Christianity in Roman Britain to AD 500*.
    London: Batsford, 1981.

_____. *Celtic Britain*. London: Thames and Hudson, 1986.

_____. *And Shall These Mute Stones Speak? Post-Roman
    Inscriptions In Western Britain*. University of Wales
    Press, 1994.

Thomas, D. R. "Hafod Adam and some Antiquities in
    Dyffryn Ceiriog." *Archaeologia Cambrensis*, 1882.

_____. *A History of the Diocese of St. Asaph*. Oswestry,
    1908-13.

Thomas, D. W. *Chwedlau a Choelion Godre'r Wyddfa*.
    Caernarfon: Gwasg Gwynedd, 1998.

Thompson, E. A. *St Germanus of Auxerre and the End of
    Roman Britain*. Boydell, 1984.

Tolstoy, Earl Nikolas. "Early British History and
    Chronology." *Transactions of the Honourable Society
    of Cymmrodorion*, 1964.

Usher [sic], Dr J. *Discourse on the Religion Anciently
    Professed by the Irish and British*. Dublin, 1815.

Ussher, Dr J. *Britannicarum Ecclesiarum Antiquitates*.
    Dublin, 1639.

Vogt, J. *The Decline of Rome*. London: Weidenfield, 1993.

Wade-Evans, The Rev. A. W. "St. Paulinus of Wales."
    Archaelologia Cambrensis 1920, p. 172.

_____. "Vortimer, Son of Vortigern." *Archaelologia Cambrensis* XCVI 1941, p. 193-195.

_____. "Further Remarks on the 'De Excidio'". *Archaelologia Cambrensis* XCVIII 1944-45, p. 120.

_____. "Prolegomena to a Study of the Lowlands." In: *Dumfreisshire and Galloway Natural History and Antiquarian Society Transactions and Journal of Proceedings* 1948-49. Third Series, Vol. XXVII, pp.62. Dumfries, 1950.

_____. "Vortigern." *Notes and Queries*, 13.5.1950.

Wales, Gerald of. *The Journey Through Wales* and *The Description of Wales*, transl. Lewis Thorpe. London: Penguin Books, 1978.

Ware, Bishop Kallistos. *The Orthodox Way*. Crestwood: St Vladimir's Seminary Press, 1999.

Wilkinson, Dr P. "A Roman baptismal bath at Bax Farm, in Kent?" In: *Current Archaeology* 237 (December 2009), pp. 8-9.

Williams, Emily Octavia. "St. Germanus, Or Garmon, Bishop of Auxerre." *Archaeologia Cambrensis* 1857, pp. 57-66.

Williams, Hugh. *Some Aspects of the Christian Church in Wales during the Fifth and Sixth Centuries*. London: The Honourable Society of Cymmrodorion, 1895.

Williams, Ifor. *Armes Prydein o Lyfr Taliesin*. Caerdydd: Gwasg Prifysgol Cymru, 1964.

_____. "Hen Chwedlau." *Trafodion Anrhydeddus Gymdeithas y Cymmrodorion*, 1946-47.

Williams, The Rev. J. "History of Radnorshire." *Archaeologia Cambrensis*, Series 3, No. 4 (1858).

Williams, Robert. "G. R.'s letter to Edward Lhuyd." *Archaeologia Cambrensis*, Series 3, No. 6 (1860).

Willis-Bund, J. W. "Some Characteristics of Welsh and Irish Saints." *Archaeologia Cambrensis* 1894, pp. 289-90.

Wilson, P. A. "Romano-British and Welsh Christianity: Continuity or Discontinuity?" In: *Welsh History Review*, 1966.

Winterbottom, M (ed.). *Gildas: The Ruin of Britain and Other Documents.* London Phillimore & Co., 1978.

Wood, I. "The End of Roman Britain: Continental Evidence and Parallels." In: Lapidge, M., and Dumville, D. (eds). *Gildas: New Approaches.* Woodbridge: The Boydell Press, 1984.

Young, Father Alexey. "A Brief Life of Blessed Augustine of Hippo 354 – 430 A.D." *Orthodox Word* 104 (May/June 1982).

Websites

www.british-history.ac.uk

www.culture.gouv.fr/culture/arcnat/auxerre/en/index

www.dot-domesday.me.uk/barbarian

www.fordham.edu/halsall/basis/columban

http://historymedren.about.com/library/text/ntxtnennius51to55.htm

www.nationaltrustnames.org.uk/Surnames.aspx

www.newadvent.org

www.outremer.co.uk/relics

www.saintpatrickdc.org

www.vortigernstudies.org.uk

www.e-gymraeg.co.uk/enwaulleoedd/amr/cronfa.aspx

www.questia.com

Sources not consulted, but referred to in the above works

Bale, John. "Comedy concernynge thre laws." *Anglia* V, 1882.

Bollandists, The Society of (eds) "Vita sancti Seueri Viennensis presbyteri et confessoris." *Analecta Bollandiana* 5, 1886.

Blair, P. H. *Roman Britain and Early England*. Edinburgh, 1963.

Camden, W. *Britannia*. London, 1594.

Caspari, C. P. *Breife, Abhandlungen und Predigten*. Christiana, 1890.

Chadwick, O. *John Cassian: A Study in Primitive Monasticism*. Cambridge: University Press, 1950.

De Plinval. "Les Campagnes de saint Germain en Grande-Bretagne contre les Pélagiens." In: *Saint Germain d'Auxerre et son Temps*. 1950.

Doble, G. H. S(t). *German of Auxerre, Patron of S. Germans, Cornwall*. 2nd edition, Shipton-on-Stour, 1928.

_____. *The Lannalet Pontifical*. Bristol, 1934.

Fowler, Rev. J.T. *The Coucher Book of Selby*. Leeds: Yorkshire Archaeological Society, 1891 a 1893.

Haslehurst, R. S. T. *The Works of Fastidius*. London, 1927.

Henderson, C. *Records of the Church and Priory of St. Germans*. 1929.

Krusch, B. (ed.) "Fredregarii et aliorum chronica." *Vitae sanctorum*. Hannover, 1888.

_____. (ed.) *Passiones vitaeque sanctorum aevi merovingici et antiquiorum aliquot*, III. Hannover, 1896.

Leland, J. *Itinerary*. Oxford, 1769.

Levison, Mohrmann, C. *The Latin of St. Patrick*. Dublin 1961.

Levison, W. (ed.), "Vita Germani." In: *Monumenta Germaniae Historica: Scriptores Rerum Merovingicrum*, 7 (Berlin, 1920).

Migne, J.-P., *Patrologia Latina*, 1844-45.

Mommsen, T. (ed.) "Prosperi Tironis Epitoma chronicum." In: *Chronica Minora Saec. IV, V, VI, VII*. Berlin 1892.

Morin, Dom. G. *Sancti Caesarii Arelatensis*, Vol II. Maretoili [Bruges]: Desclée, 1942.

Narbey, L'Abbé. *Etude critique sur la vie de S. Germain*. Paris, 1884.

Pickens, W. M. M. "St. German of Cornwall's Day." *Devon and Cornwall Notes and Queries* XXVII Part V (January 1957).

Royal Commission on Historical Manuscripts: *Report on Manuscripts in the Welsh Language*, Volume 1. London: HMSO, 1898-1910.

Schoel, C. W. *De Ecclesiasticae Britonum Scotorumque Historiae Fontibus*. Berlin: W. Hertz, 1851.

Schuets-Miller, M. K. "Survival of Early Christian Symbolism in Monastic Churches of New Spain and Visions of the Millennial Kingdom." *Journal of the Southwest*, 42 (2000).

Surius, Laurentius. *De probatis Sanctorum historiis*, Köln, 1570-75.

St Germanus: timeline (dates AD)

Approximate dates italicized

Church	State
150 Justin Martyr lists lands in which Christians are found. Britain not included.	
180 Irenaeus of Lyons lists churches known to him. Britain not mentioned.	Commodus succeeds Marcus Aurelius as Emperor.
200 Athanasius and Origen suggest presence of Christians in Britain.	209-212 Septimus Severus campaigns in northern Britain.
250, 257-260 Christians severely persecuted.	235-285 Severe civil and military unrest.
260-302 Christianity tolerated to a degree, and expands rapidly.	260-274 "Gallic Empire" of Postumus in Gaul and Britain.
	296 Constantius regains Britain from Allectus.
303-305 Renewed persecution of Christians. *304* Martyrdom of Alban.	305 Renewal of civil war.
	306 Constantine the Great declared Augustus by Roman army in Britain.
c. 311 St Anthony becomes a hermit.	
	312 Constantine the Great defeats Maxentius at the Milvian Bridge, and wins Rome.
313 *Edict of Milan* brings official end to persecution of Christians in western part of Empire.	313 Licinius defeats Maximinus and becomes Constantine's co-emperor in the East.

Church	State
314 Clerics from Britain present at Synod of Arles.	314 Constantine seizes most of Europe from Licinius.
335 St Athanasius the Great banished to Trier.	324-337 Constantine the Great defeats Licinius, and becomes sole ruler. Constantinople founded as capital city of eastern part of Roman Empire.
347 British bishops present at Council of Sofia.	
350 Pelagius born in Britain.	350-361 Constantius II sole ruler of Roman Empire.
357 *Life of St Anthony* published by St Athanasius	357 Julian the Apostate defeats Alemanni at Strasbourg.
358/9 St Hilary of Poitiers praises British bishops for their Orthodoxy.	
359 British bishops present at Council of Rimini.	359 Constantinople becomes capital of entire Roman Empire.
	360-64 Picts, Saxons and others attack Britain.
	368 Theodosius defeats both barbarians and Valentius' rebellion in Britain.
	370 Huns defeat Alans on east European steppes. Alans flee westwards.
	370 Birth of Vortigern.
370-379 St Basil the Great bishop of Caesarea. Monasticism spreads to the West. 378 Birth of St Germanus in Auxerre.	378 Romans severely defeated by Visigoths at Adrianople: the Emperor Valens killed.

Church	State
380 Edict of Thessalonica: Catholicism enshrined as sole state religion of Empire.	
382-385 St Jerome in Rome.	382 Magnus Maximus defeats Picts and Scots in north Britain.
	383 Revolt of Magnus Maximus: troops withdrawn from Britain to the European continent.
386 Pelagius decides upon a career in the Church. St Jerome at Bethlehem.	
387 Death of St Heladius, Bishop of Auxerre. Succeeded by Amator.	
	388 Magnus Maximus defeated by Theodosius the Great and executed.
	390 Birth of Galla Placidia, daughter of Theodosius the Great.
391 Paganism outlawed.	
394 Pelagius a monk, according to St Jerome.	392-395 Theodsius the Great sole ruler.
395-430 Augustine bishop of Hippo.	395-423 Honorius emperor in the West.
396 Victricius, Bishop of Rouen, visits Britain.	396-402 Stilicho defeats several attacks by Visigoths under Alaric.
397 *Life of St Martin* published by Sulpicius Severus, and a small church built above St Martin's grave.	

Church	State
397 Death of St Ambrose, Bishop of Milan.	
400 Pope Anastasius and Emperor Honorius condemn Origenism.	398-400 Barbarians again attack Britain. Stilicho recovers Britain from Magnus Maximus' successors, and takes soldiers from thence to defend Italy.
	401 Alans, Swabians and Vandals invade Rhaetia (South Bavaria \ Switzerland), but are defeated by Stilicho. Alaric the Goth invades Italy.
402 St John Chrysostom praises British bishops for their Orthodoxy.	402 Honorius moves the Empire's western capital from Milan to Ravenna.
405-410 Birth of Faustus of Riez	
	406 Alans, Swabians and Vandals flood from Germany into Gaul. 406-7 The army in Britain elects a series of rebel leaders. One of them, styled Constantine III, withdraws soldiers from Britain to invade continent. 408 Honorius orders execution of Stilicho. 408/410 Britain devastated by Saxons.
	409 Zosimus mentions rebellion in Armorica. Inhabitants of Britain declare independence from Rome.

Church	State
410 Pelagius' *Commentary on the Epistles of St Paul*. Pelagius and Caelestius flee Rome, and arrive at Carthage.	410 Asked for military aid, Honorius tells cities of Britain to look to their own defence. Rome taken and sacked by Visigoths.
411 Pelagius leaves Carthage for Palestine.	411 Constantine III defeated and executed.
415 Blessèd Augustine attacks Pelagianism, devising the doctrine of Predestination. Synods of Jerusalem and Disopolis declare Pelagius to be Orthodox. *415* Birth of Constantius of Lyons	
416 Synods of African and Numidian bishops condemn Pelagianism.	416 Galla Placidia, daughter of Theodosius, arrives in Ravenna.
417 - 418 Pope Innocent severs Pelagius' communion with the Church in the West. Innocent succeeded by Zosimus, who declares Pelagius and Caelesius to be Orthodox. Riots in Rome result in Emperor Honorius outlawing Pelagianism, and Zosimus follows suit. St Jerome's *Dialogue against the Pelagians*. ?Death of Pelagius. Rutilius Namantianus mentions presence of anchorites by Tyrrhenian Sea.	417 Exuperantius defeats rebels in Armorica.

Church	State
417-418 Death of Amator, Bishop of Auxerre: Germanus ordained in his place.	418 Visigoths settled in Aquitaine.
421 Celestinus I ordained Pope.	420s First Germanic settlements in Kent.
425 Decree against Pelagianism republished by Emperor Valentinian. 425 Leoporius of Trêves renounces Pelagianism.	425 Aëtius comes into power in western Empire. Valentinian III emperor in the West. Vortigern ("Great King") ruler of Britain.
429 Pelagianism in Britain: St Germanus' first visit. Hilarius ordained Metropolitan of Arles. Caelestius the Pelagian in Constantinople. Palladius ordained bishop of the Christian Irish.	429 Vandals establish independent kingdom in North Africa.
430 Theodosius II expels Pelagians from Constantinople. Easter 430: Hallelujah Victory: Germanus defeats combined Picts and Saxons.	
431 Ecumenical Council of Ephesus condemns Nestorianism and Pelagianism.	
432 Death of Pope Celestinus I	
433 Faustus ordained Abbot of Lérins	
	435 Begining of Tibatto's rebellion in Armorica.

Church	State
	435 Burgundians defeated near Worms.
437 ?St Germanus' second visit to Britain, accompanied by Severus. ?Honorius' edict against Pelagianism in force in Britain. ?Death of St Germanus.	437 Battle between "Vitalinus" (?Vortigern) and Ambrosius Aurelianus at "Guoloph" (?Wallop, Hampshire). Aëtius effectively governor of western Empire. Valentinian III sails from Rome to Constantinople. Sigisvult consul. Litorus defeats Tibatto in Armorica.
	439/442 Saxons of Kent rebel against Vortigern.
440-461 Leo I, Pope of Rome, frustrates attempts of Hilary of Arles and other Gallic bishops to establish an independent Patriarchate of Gaul.	441 Commentators in Gaul write that part of Britain is in Saxon hands. 441 ?Death of Vortigern.
445/48 ?St Germanus' second visit to Britain, accompanied by Severus. ?Honorius' edict against Pelagianism in force in Britain. ?Death of St Germanus.	443-450 Plague strikes Britain and parts of continental Europe.
446 Severus ordained Bishop of Trier	446/454 Britons appeal unsuccessfully to Aëtius for military aid.
	447 ? Death of Vortigern.
449 Death of Hilarius of Arles.	449 Aëtius defeats Huns at Châlons-sur-Marne

Church	State
450 The "Chronicler of Gaul" records Predestination to be a "heresy" of Augustine's.	450 Vortimer, son of Vortigern, defeats Saxons at Richborough. Death of Galla Placidia *450/455* Renewed Saxon campaign: Kingdom of Kent established.
451 Council of Chalcedon.	451 Aëtius defeats Huns at Catalaunian Fields.
	455 Aëtius executed on orders of Valentinian III, who is in turn murdered in Rome. Vandals sack Rome. Last mention of Vortigern in the Anglo-Saxon Chronicle. *455* ?Death of Vortigern and/or Vortimer. *455-485* Series of British victories temporarily checks Saxon expansion.
462 Faustus, Abbot of Lérins, ordained Bishop of Riez.	
470 Sidonius Apollinaris ordained Bishop of Clermont-Ferrand.	
471 Sidonius Apollinaris mentions Riocatus the Briton.	
475 Death of Severus of Trier. *475/80* Constantius of Lyons writes *Life of St Germanus*.	476 Deposition of Romulus Augustulus ends Roman Empire in West.
	481 Euric the Visigoth conquers Provence.
485 Birth of Gildas.	*485* Victory of Britons at battle of *Mons Badonicus* halts further Saxon expansion for decades.

Church	State
	486 Franks led by Clovis defeat Syagrius, and take Auxerre.
490/493 Death of Faustus of Riez. 498 Clovis baptized: Franks become Catholic.	493-526 Theoderic the Goth master of Italy. 496 Clovis defeats Alemanni.
500 Reverentius mentions Germanus in his *Life of Hillarius of Arles*.	500 Theoderic in Rome.
529 Synods of Orange and Valence condemn St John Cassian's teachings regarding Predestination.	529 Justinian closes Plato's Academy.
545–549 Gildas writes his *Destruction of Britain*: makes no mention of St Germanus.	542-49 Plague sweeps into Britain and Ireland from the continent: resistance to Saxons seriously weakened. Before 545: Clotild, wife of Clovis, has a church built on the site of Germanus' tomb.
573 – 603 Stephanus Africanus composes a *Life of St Amator*. 597 Augustine arrives at Canterbury.	577 Battle of Dyrham: Saxons take Gloucester, Cirencester and Bath from Britons. *590/600* Battle of Catterick: Britons defeated by Anglian Northumbrians.
	613 Battle of Chester: Anglian victory over Britons. Monks of Bangor Iscoed slain, and monastery destroyed.
640 Pope John IV reminds Church in Ireland that Pelagianism is a heresy.	636-639 Arabs invade Syria, Palestine and North Africa.

Church	State
	715 Suavaricus, Bishop of Auxerre, establishes an independent princedom there.
725 First reference to monastery of Saint-Germain in Auxerre.	726 Leo III orders destruction of all icons.
796-830 Nennius writes *History of the Britons*, mentioning St Germanus' visit. 817 Rule of St Benedict adopted at monastery of Saint-Germain	793 First Viking raid on Britain strikes monastery of Lindisfarne. 795 Vikings raid Iona.
800-825 Pillar of Eliseg mentions St Germanus.	800 Charlemagne crowned Emperor.
	812 Fort of Deganwy struck by lightning and burnt.
840 Conrad, uncle of King Charles the Bald, miraculously healed before St Germanus' tomb. Orders building of new church to display the saint's relics, which are moved there in August 841 in the presence of the king.	843 Restoration of icons.
859 Conrad installs St Germanus' relics in the church's crypt.	860 Russians attack Constantinople.
873-75 Hericus of Auxerre composes metrical *Life* of St Germanus, and prose *Miracles of St Germanus*.	879 Basil I defeats Arabs and reconquers Cappadocia.
	887-89 Vikings attack Auxerre and its abbey.

Church	State
	909 Géron, Bishop of Auxerre, defeats Vikings.
	1003-05 King Robert the Pious besieges and takes Auxerre
1030 St Germanus' relics clothed in silk.	
1099-1107 Monastery of Saint-Germain comes under control of Cluny.	1099 first Crusade captures Jerusalem.
1136 Geoffrey of Monmouth writes *History of the Kings of Britain*, mentioning Germanus and Lupus.	
1256 Monastery of Saint-Germain regains independence.	1261 Constantinople liberated by Michael VIII.
1277-1360 St Germanus' Abbey rebuilt in Gothic style.	1347-1351 Bubonic plague ravages Europe.
1358 Relics of St Germanus placed in Exeter Cathedral.	
1480 Mombritius (in Milan) publishes *Life* of St Germanus in his *Sanctuarium*.	1480 Battle of Ugra River: Muscovy wins independence from Golden Horde.
1567 St Germanus' relics at Auxerre lost.	1567 Huguenot forces take and despoil Auxerre.
1570-75 Laurentius Surius publishes version of the *Life of St Germanus* in Cologne.	1571 Turks conquer Cyprus. 1572 Massacre of Huguenots at Paris.
1577 Term "Semi-Pelagianism" coined.	1577 Peace of Bergerac ends 4th French War of Religion.
1639 Ussher names Maes Garmon by Mold as site of the Hallelujah Victory.	1639 Russian Cossacks advance over Urals to Okhotsk.

Church	State
1647 Séan Mac Colgan's *Triadis Thaumaturga* mentions Germanus \ Mogorman \ Mogornan son of Restitutus of Brittany, Bishop of Man.	1641-49 Irish Confederate Wars: native Irish social and religious order destroyed. 1647 English Puritans forbid celebration of Christmas.
1739 Memorial raised at Maes Garmon.	1739 Treaty of Belgrade ends Russo-Turkish War.
	1789 French Revolution.
1791 Property of Auxerre clerics sold by Revolutionary Government.	1791 Champ de Mars Massacre in Paris.
1811 Western part of Saint-Germain abbey church demolished.	1811 Podil quarter of Kiev destroyed by fire.
1884 Version of *Life of St Germanus* published in Paris.	1884-5 Berlin Conference: Africa partitioned between European powers.
	1917 October Revolution begins Communist rule in Russia and beyond.
1920 Levison edits standard text of *Life of St Germanus*.	1920 League of Nations Covenant. Hitler outlines National Socialist programme.

Appendix I:
David of Wales and Germanus of Auxerre.

The first mention of St Germanus of Auxerre in a context in which St David also figures prominently is the vaticinatory poem, *Armes Prydain Fawr* ("The Great Prophecy of Britiain"). It was probably composed by a south Wales monk, possibly in south-west Wales, about the years 930-937,[1] and prophesies that a confederation of the Welsh and other nations, including the Irish and Dublin Vikings, will unite to rout the English and drive them out of Britain.

Lines 129-132 of the *Armes* foresee that the Welsh, under the banner of St David, will lead the Irish and the "heathens of Dublin" into battle against the English, destroying them utterly. Then lines 145-146 state that:

"Ef talha6r o ana6r Garma6n garant
y pedeir blyned ar petwar cant."

*"With the help of the kinsmen of Garmon [Germanus],
the four years and the four hundred will be paid for."*

The 404 years being reckoned from the first landing of the English in Britain to the date of the poem's composition, according to the author's reckoning.[2] Lines 147-148, immediately following this mention of Germanus, read:

"G6yr g6ychyr g6allt hirion, ergyrdofyd,
Y dihol Saesson o Iwerdon dybyd."

"Splendid, long-haired men, skilful in assault,

226

Will come from Ireland to drive out the English. "

If the author was writing in south-west Wales, he could well have known that the Welsh name of Wexford, in south-east Ireland (almost directly opposite St Davids), was "Llwch Garmawn".[3] Given that, and the mention of the Irish both before and immediately after the reference to Germanus, it could be conjectured that the poet's "kinsmen of Garmawn" are the men of Leinster.

However, it is also possible that the "kinsmen of Germanus" were the men of Powys, in central and north-eastern Wales. It was a realm whose rulers had been associated with St Germanus since at least the beginning of the 9th century (and probably long previous to that), as both Nennius and the Eliseg's Pillar inscription testify.

This invocation of the name of Germanus could, then, be seen as the poet's attempt to expand the envisioned anti-English confederation beyond south-west Wales: but if so, was he drawing on traditions other than Constantius' biography? Because in addition to Constantius' Germanus, the ascetic bishop, diplomat and military leader, there exists Nennius's legendary Germanus, who hounded Vortigern to his doom, destroyed Benlli the Giant, and established Cadell as King of Powys.

Either Germanus would be a valuable intercessor on the day of battle, but the author of the "Armes" doesn't suggest any particular bond or association between David and Germanus. The author invokes the spiritual aid of God, St David and the "saints of Britain": but St Germanus only by virtue of the military prowess of his "kinsmen", and there's no appeal for his aid.

About the year 1092, Rhygyfarch composed a Latin *Vita S. Dauid* based, he tells us, on older documents.[4] Rhygyfarch states therein that David was taught by Paulinus, who had himself been taught by Saint Germanus of Auxerre. As stated in Chapter 10 of the *Vita:*

> "*After that he went to the scholar Paulinus, a disciple of the holy bishop Germanus...*"[5]

In Chapter 49, the spectre of heresy raises its head once again, despite St Germanus' previous efforts:

"*Since the Pelagian heresy was reviving – inserting its obstinate strength in the inmost parts of our country like the poison of a venomous snake, even after Saint Germanus had come to help a second time...*"[6]

Therefore a great synod was held at Brefi in order to tackle the subject. So numerous was the crowd, the debate could not be heard. Clothing was piled high for the Catholic preachers to stand upon, but the well of their inspiration ran dry, and their efforts at speaking came to naught. Then Paulinus suggested that David should be fetched from Mynyw. He came reluctantly, but was persuaded by Deiniol and Dyfrig: and on his way to Brefi, he revived a widow's dead son.

He performed another miracle when he arrived at the synod, the ground rising beneath his feet so that he was elevated, and could be clearly heard. As a result, Pelagianism was expelled from the land (*Heresis*

228

expellitur...). David was made an archbishop, and the *Vita* again states that the heresy was driven out (*Expulsa igitur heresi*). The decisions of the Brefi synod were confirmed and amended at a later synod, the "Synod of Victory" (*synodus, qui nomen Victorię*).

The Welsh version of David's *Vita*, in the Llanddewi Brefi Anchorite's Book (1346)[7] mentions neither Germanus (stating that Paulinus was taught by "a holy bishop in Rome") nor Pelagianism.

Rhygyfarch composed the *Vita* in response to a perceived need to establish the primacy of St Davids at a time when the influence of Canterbury, and the military might of the Normans, were making themselves felt in south Wales. To establish such a claim required historical proof in the form of documents: no simple matter in a culture which may have depended largely on oral tradition, and where time, neglect and he depredations of the Vikings had largely erased whatever written testimony had once existed.

The period, therefore, saw a flowering of historical research aimed at "the unearthing of lost or forgotten charters and the traditions of saintly founders...and (especially in Wales) Lives of the saints".[8] If St Davids was to contend for metropolitan status, a written work setting forth its patron saint's virtues, and his connection with all parts of the diocesan territory, would have been deemed indispensable.

The suspicion that Rhygyfarch could have derived part of his account, notably that of the Brefi synod and the

"Synod of Victory", from Constantius' *Life of St Germanus*, is no novelty. As Nora Chadwick wrote:

"...we may well suspect that Rhigyfarch is echoing the two anti-Pelagian campaigns ascribed to St Germanus, to whom he has referred immediately before...our only authority for such synods...reads suspiciously like an echo of Constantius' Life of St Germanus, a work by which Rhigyfarch would seem to be directly influenced." [9]

The present writer proposes to explore further the possibility that the "oldest manuscripts... worn along the sides and backs by the continual gnawing of worms and the damage of the passing years", which Rhygyfarch states he had at hand, included a copy of Conatantius' *Vita sancti Germani*, or a work which conflated elements of the *vitae* of both David and Germanus.

Let us consider:

1) Constantius' *Life of Saint Germanus of Auxerre*, the *prima vita*, contains the following passage:

   "...but he was constantly thronged by the crowds that came out to meet him, so much so, that every eminence associated with his journey is to this day crowned by a chapel, a hermit's cell, or a cross erected where he prayed or taught." [10]

   Thus our earliest knowledge of Germanus associates him with "eminences", upon which he prayed or taught.

2) As Christ's faithful disciples, it could be expected that both David and Germanus could revive the dead, including young men (Luke 7:11-17, Acts 20:9-12). Both perform that specific miracle whilst away from home. Germanus, in Ravenna following his journey to the Emperor's court, stretches himself out on the dead body (cf. III Kings 17:21, IV Kings 4:34, 35) "with many prayers and tears", as Constantius says. David, on his journey to Brefi, prays for the revival of the widow's son, whilst being close enough to the corpse to wet its face with his tears (*faciem lacrimis rigauit*, chapter 51), according to Rhygyfarch.

3) Germanus successfully challenged the Pelagians by preaching at a public assembly, but a second effort was needed to put the matter beyond doubt. David did likewise, but a subsequent synod was necessary to seal the issue.

4) In both cases, clothing is mentioned in connection with a lack of eloquence. For all their "rich attire", the Pelagians' words dry up before Germanus: and at Brefi, the Catholics' preaching is futile, despite the heaping up of a mound of clothing which Dewi declines to climb. Rather, a hill rises miraculously under his feet, and a church is subsequently built upon it (see 1 above).[11]

5) Germanus wins the "Hallelujah Victory". David's work is crowned at the "Synod of Victory".

The present writer knows of no surviving account or

tradition to the effect that the earth rose beneath Germanus' feet. However, Camden records the following tradition concerning St Albans in his *Britannia*:

"…ut inquit Beda, operis in eius memoriam poserunt, & tanta religionis opinio Verolano accessit, ut hic Synodus anno mundi redempti CCCCXXIX haberetur, cum Pelagina hæresis per Agricolam Seueriani episcopi filium in hac insula pullulasset, Britannicasque ecclesias ita maculsset, ut ad veritatem afferendam (*or* asserendam) Germanum Antisiodorensum, & Lupum Tricassinum e Gallia Euocarent; qui refutata hæresi se venerabiles Britannis reddiderunt, imprimus Germanus, qui plurima per hanc insulam templa sibi sacrata habet, & in ipsa huius prostratis urbis area, Germani sacellum[12] etiam num super est, qui loci ille pro suggestu verbum diuinum effetus erat, ut antiquae fane Albani membranulæ testantur."[13]

Which is interpreted as follows: that there yet remained in Camden's time, above or near to [*super*] the levelled ruins of the Roman city of Verulanium, a chapel dedicated in the name of Germanus, who in this island has many churches consecrated in his name: in which very place he preached the divine word from a mound/platform/stage/tribune, as ancient manuscripts of St Alban's church do testify.

Pro suggestu may be translated as "on the platform".[14] *Super* suggests, and *pro suggestu* confirms, that the saint is preaching from an eminence.

The reader's attention is drawn to the following places in Wales:

- "Pall Garmon" (Germanus' Pulpit/ Throne/ Platform), the prehistoric long barrow at Capel Garmon near Llanrwst; [15]
- "Tomen / Twmpath Garmon" (Germanus' Mound) by Llanfechain (Llanarmon ym Mechain) church;
- "Boncyn / Twmpath Garmon" (Germanus' Mound) by Llanarmon Dyffryn Ceiriog church;
- "Bryngarmon" (Germanus' Hill) by Maes Garmon (Germanus' Field) near Mold;
- Castle Caereinion church, dedicated in the name of Germanus and in whose yard stands a mound supposedly connected with the saint; and
- "Bedd Garmon" (Germanus' Grave), a prehistoric burial mound near the parish of Saint Harmons in Gwytheyrnion. The latter is close to Llanddewi Brefi, both places being "in the depths of our land" (to use Rhygyfarch's phrase), in the north-easternmost part of the Diocese of St Davids.

Such mounds may originally have been prehistoric burial barrows, later utilized or heightened for preaching or other purposes. They may be the remains of fortifications, or have had forts built upon them, as at Castle Caereinion and, possibly, Llanarmon yn Iâl.

They could also have been built, or subsequently utilized, as the local *twmpath chwarae* (literally, "play mound") where games, dances and other entertainments were conducted. As Robert Llwyd observed:

"Rhai a redant i butteinia ar y suliau, rhai i'r twmpath chwareu, ac i ddawnsio..."[16]

(*Some run a-whoring on Sundays, some to the twmpath chwarae, and to dancing...*)

Ellis Wynne, likewise:

"A chynta peth a welwn i, yn f'ymyl *dwmpath chwareu*, â'r fath gâd-gamlan mewn Peisieu gleision a Chapieu cochion, yn dawnsio 'n hoew-brysur."[17]

(*And the first thing I saw beside me was a twmpath chwarae, with such a milling mob in blue petticoats and red caps, dancing vigorously.*)

Those familiar with Welsh history know that such merriment often took place in the local churchyard (to the disgust of reformers), and one could expect to find *twmpathau chwarae* in such places: as at Pennant Melangell, possibly, amongst others.

Defence, burial and entertainment are all plausible origins of these mounds, but do not, in themselves, explain a specific original or subsequent connection with Saint Germanus in popular memory. It may be worth noting that the association of a personal name with the Welsh place-name "poncen", "twmpath" or "tomen" (mound, hummock, pile) is most rare. A single Bonc Fadog is attested in Anglesey,[18] but all other instances known to the writer bear the name of Germanus, and are evidence of a strong connection, in and around the territory of the ancient Kingdom of Powys, between this saint alone and mounds of one description or another.

Bearing in mind what Constantius and Camden wrote, and knowing of the strength of Germanus' association with Powys (as evidenced by the numerous churches dedicated in his name, other place-names containing the element "Garmon", and the Eliseg's Pillar inscription), it may not be unreasonable to suggest that:

- There existed a tradition, originating in his *Vita* and initially associated (in Britain) with St Albans, that Germanus had stood on a hillock or raised structure when preaching against the heretics.
- A legend then evolved that the ground under Germanus' feet had risen as he preached, this signifying divine approval.
- His legend was translocated to Powys, becoming connected with Germanus churches in, or near to, that kingdom.
- The legend subsequently migrated (as tales do) to the adjacent Diocese of St Davids, where Rhygyfarch, or a predecessor to whose writings Rhygyfarch had access, grafted it onto what was known of the life of St David.

It could conceivably have been Rhygyfarch or his predecessor's intention to use elements of a notable saint's *vita* to pad out his depiction of David: but with so many such *vitae* available, why choose Germanus'? Was it because of doubts concerning David's orthodoxy, and that there were aspects of his behaviour and practices which could be viewed as tending to Pelagianism? Was it in order to disarm any such accusation that Rhygyfarch depicted David campaigning against Pelagianism, by borrowing elements from the *Life* that most well-known anti-Pelagian, Germanus of Auxerre?[19]

Subsequent to the publication of Rhygyfarch's account, we find the same motif of the earth rising under a preaching saint in Jocelyn of Furness' *Life of St Kentigern*:

> "And when he had, by the instruction and dictation of the Spirit, taught much that referred to the Christian faith, in the place which is called Holdelm, the ground on which he sat, in the sight of all, grew into a little hill, and remaineth there unto this day;" [20]

which resulted in the conversion and baptism of many. The Breviary of Aberdeen (early 16th-century, but derived from much earlier material) gives a slightly different account of this miracle: on Kentigern's return to Glasgow, so great a multitude come to greet him that his preaching could scarcely be heard. Whereupon the ground on which he stood rose up in a hillock, so that all could see and hear him. As with Germanus in St Albans, a "notable chapel" (*insignis capella*), dedicated in his name, was built there (*iuxta Glasgu*).[21]

Also, the Welsh poet Gwilym Gwyn (fl. c.1560-?1600) composed an ode to St Eilian containing the following passage:

> "He taught a task to nine bishops whilst being attired; in a small [area of] land, on the *awria* hillock, [in] most excellent language was his good sermon. Two people whom he raised from death to

236

life before [the lapse of] two hours [enjoyed] a great destiny [thereby]; the multitude in the church, thousands [of them] esteemed Eilian highly, after receiving belief and baptism and turning to the way of the teacher of the faith...[22]

These accounts are highly interesting in the present context. Kentigern and Eilian are preaching to those who are not of the True Faith, and who are consequently converted. The earth beneath Kentigern rises into a hillock, and Eilian preaches from a hillock of some description, though the adjective *awria* remains obscure. Eilian also raises two persons from the dead: and as in Constantius' account of Germanus' confrontation with the Pelagians, Eilian is depicted as lecturing men of importance, i.e. nine bishops, whilst he is "being attired". Once again, the matter of clothing is thought worthy of mention.

Elements of both Jocelyn and Gwilym Gwyn's accounts may, therefore, testify to the enduring influence of Constantius' *Vita Germani,* be that direct or, more likely, indirect via Rhygyfarch's *Vita S. Dauid* or other works no longer extant. A thousand and more years after Constantius described the contest between Germanus and the gorgeously-attired Pelagians, and five hundred years after Rhygyfarch related David's feat at the Synod of Brefi, we may have, in Gwilym Gwyn's ode, the last glimmer of a tradition that a famous saint "taught a lesson" to "bishops", that he stood on a mound, and that clothing had a part to play.[23]

Early 15th-century belief in an indirect connection

between David and Germanus is expressed in Bibliothèque National (Paris) MS lat. 17294, where the first breviary lesson for the Feast of St David states:

> "Cum sanctus Germanus predicaret in Britannia contra heresum Pelagiam, iam beatum Patriciun sibi ad familiare contubernium sociauit. Qui cum occiduos partes Wallie pertransiret, tandem ad locum amenum et sibi gratum, qui Wallis Rosina nuncupatur, peruenit..." [24]

> *"While St Germanus was preaching in Britain against the Pelagian heresy, he admitted St Patrick into his fellowship. Passing through the western part of Wales, he arrived at length at a pleasant and for him acceptable place called Rose Valley..."*

Which is, of course, the very place divinely ordained for St David, Patrick being redirected to Ireland. As O. T. Edwards observes, the mention of St Germanus and Pelagianism"...would immediately have sparked off associations...with St David, who was credited with having stamped it out."[25] St Germanus is depicted as a mitred bishop in a miniature at the lower left-hand corner of folio 426v. of the manuscript, apparently preaching to, amongst others, a man who may be Sant of Ceredigion, St David's father.

Notes

1. Williams, Ifor. *Armes Prydein o Lyfr Taliesin.* Caerdydd: Gwasg Prifysgol Cymru, 1964, tt. xvii, xx-xxii.

2. Isaac, G. R. "Armes Prydain Fawr and St David." In: Evans, J.W., and Wooding, J. M. (eds): *St David of Wales: Cult, Church and Nation.* Woodbridge: The Boydell Press, 2007, pp. 161-181. The text and translation followed is that of G. R. Issac, pp. 178-179.

3. Wexford, now known as *Loch Garman* in Irish, is called "Llwch Garmon" in *Brut y Tywysogion* and "Llwch Garmawn" in *Historia Gruffud vab Kenan.* According to O'Donovan, however, the place was anciently Loch Carman: see Goddard, H. O. "Aenach Carman: Its Site." In: *Journal of the Royal Society of Antiquaries of Ireland*, Vol. 36, No. 1 (1906), pp. 11-12. It's likely, therefore, that the name is not derived from that of St Germanus, but that the proximity of Wales, the familiarity of the saint's name, and Welsh influence in Ireland may have led to the recasting of "Carman" as "Garman".

4. James, J. W. *Rhygyfarch's Life of St. David.* Cardiff: University of Wales Press, 1967, xi. Also: Davies, J. R. "Some Observations on the 'Nero', 'Digby' and 'Vespasian' Recensions of *Vita S. David*." In: Evans and Wooding, pp. 156-160.

    The *Vita S. Dauid* quotations and chapter numbers are as according to Sharpe, R., and Davies, J. R. Davies. "Rhygyfarch's *Life* of St David", in Evans and Wooding, pp. 107-155. One wonders whether Rhygyfarch, in bemoaning the sorry state his sources, had in mind the words of Pionius, rescriber of the 4th -century *Martyrdom of Polycarp*? For Pionius, too, recorded that "time had nearly turned [the manuscripts] to rags, but I carefully gathered them together, hoping that the Lord Jesus Christ will likewise gather me unto his elect...".

5. *Exinde perrexit ad Paulinum scribam, discipulum sancti Germani episcopi...*

6. *Quia uero post sancti Germani secundo auxilia Pelagiana heresis, suęobstinationis neruos, ueluti uenenosi serpentis uirus, intimis patrię compaginibus inserens, reuiuiscetbat...*

This may be compared with Chapter 12 of Gildas' *De Excidio* where, in excoriating Arianism, he writes:

...donec arriana perfidia, atrox ceu anguis, transmarina nobis euomens uenena fratres in unum habitantes exitiabiliter faceret seiungi, ac sic quasi uia facta trans oceanum omnes omnino bestiae ferae mortiferum cuiuslibet haeresos uirus horrido ore uibrantes letalia dentium uulnera patriae...

[...until the Arian unbelief, fierce as a serpent spewing upon us its foreign poison, caused deadly separation between brethren dwelling together. Thus, as if a path were made across the ocean, all kinds of wild beasts began, with horrid mouths, to inject the fatal poison of every manner of heresy, and to inflict the lethal wounds of their teeth upon a country...]

Could Gildas' "every manner of heresy" include Pelagianism? If so, he mentions it nowhere else.

7. Evans, D. S. *The Welsh Life of St David*. Cardiff: University of Wales Press, 1988.
8. Brooke, C. "The Archbishops of St David's, Llandaff and Caerleon-on-Usk." In: Chadwick, N. K. (ed.), *Studies in the Early British Church*. Cambridge: University Press, 1958, p. 213-214.
9. Chadwick, N. K. "Intellectual Life in West Wales in the Last Days of the Celtic Church." In: Chadwick, N. K. (ed.), *Studies in the Early British Church*. Cambridge: University Press, 1958, p. 139.
10. Hoare, F. R. (tr.) "Constantius of Lyon: The Life of Saint Germanus of Auxerre." In: *Soldiers of Christ: Saints and Saints' Lives from Late Antiquity and the Early Middle Ages*, eds. T. F. X. Noble and T. Head. New York: Sheed & Ward, 1995, pp. 75-106.
11. Chapter 52: *Iubent constructum uestibus cumulum conscendere, at ille recusauit...terra sub ipso accrescens attollitur in collem...in cuius collis cacumine ecclesia sita est.*
12. *Sacellum*: small monumental chapel, unroofed enclosure with small altar, funerary chapel or small roofless shrine.
13. Camden, W. *Britannia; sive Florentissimorum Regnorum, Angliae, Scotiae, Hiberniae... descriptio.* Francofurdi [Frankfurt], 1590.
14. Smith, W., and Hall, T.D. *A Copious and Critical English-Latin Dictionary*. New York: American Book Co., 1871, p.516.
15. E. Lhuyd, MS Bodleian Rawlinson B.464 fol.9 (*Parochialia*), has as follows:

    Y palh oedh gynt wrth Gappel Garmon. Mem. Gerrig ar i penne yn y dhaiar mewn lhe a elwir

Ogo y Ty'n y Koed.
(*The "pall" was formerly by Capel Garmon. Mem. Stones standing on end in the ground at a place called Ty'n y Coed Cave.*)

The identification of "Pall Garmon" with the Capel Garmon barrow is confirmed on page 323 of the Rev. Ellis Davies' *The Prehistoric & Roman Remains of Denbighshire*, Cardiff 1929.

16. *Llwybr Hyffordd yn cyfarwydd[o] yr anghyfarwydd i'r nefoedd*, 1630.
17. *Gweledigaetheu y Bardd Cwsc*, 1703. See further references under "twmpath" in *Geiriadur Prifysgol Cymru*, Caerdydd 1999 – 2002, Vol. 4, page 3659.
18. Tregaean (Anglesey) Land Tax Assessment, 1815.
19. Wooding, J. M. "The figure of David." In: Evans, J.W., and Wooding, J. M. (eds): *St David of Wales: Cult, Church and Nation*. Woodbridge: The Boydell Press, 2007, p. 17.
20. Forbes, A. P., *Lives of St Ninian and St Kentigern* (Historians of Scotland, Vol. 5) 1874, p.93. Facsimile reprint, Llanerch, 1989.
21. Jackson, K. H. "The Sources for the Life of St Kentigern." In: Chadwick, N. K. (ed.) *Studies in the Early British Church*. Cambridge: University Press, 1958, p. 319.
22. Ap Huw, Maredudd. *A Critical Examination of Welsh Poetry relating to the Native Saints of North Wales (c.1350-1670)*. Unpublished PhD dissertation, Oxford 2001.
23. It may also be worth remembering that according to Constantius, St Germanus was constantly attended by six bishops during his stay in

Ravenna.
24. Edwards, O. T. "The Office of St David in Paris, Bibliothèque Nationale, MS lat. 17294." In: Evans, J. W., and Wooding, J. M. (eds.) *St David of Wales: Cult, Church and Nation.* Woodbridge: Boydell Press, 2007, p.244.
25. *ibid.*, p.245.

Map 1: The Roman Empire in the West c. 400AD

Map 2: Gaul in St Germanus' Time

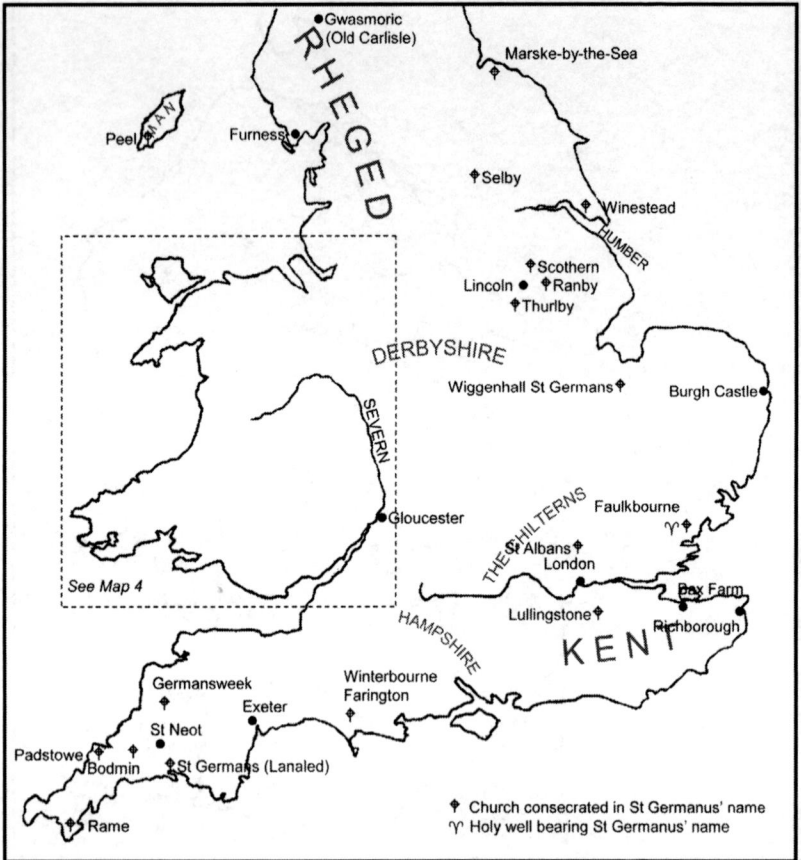

Map 3: Traces of St Germanus in Britain

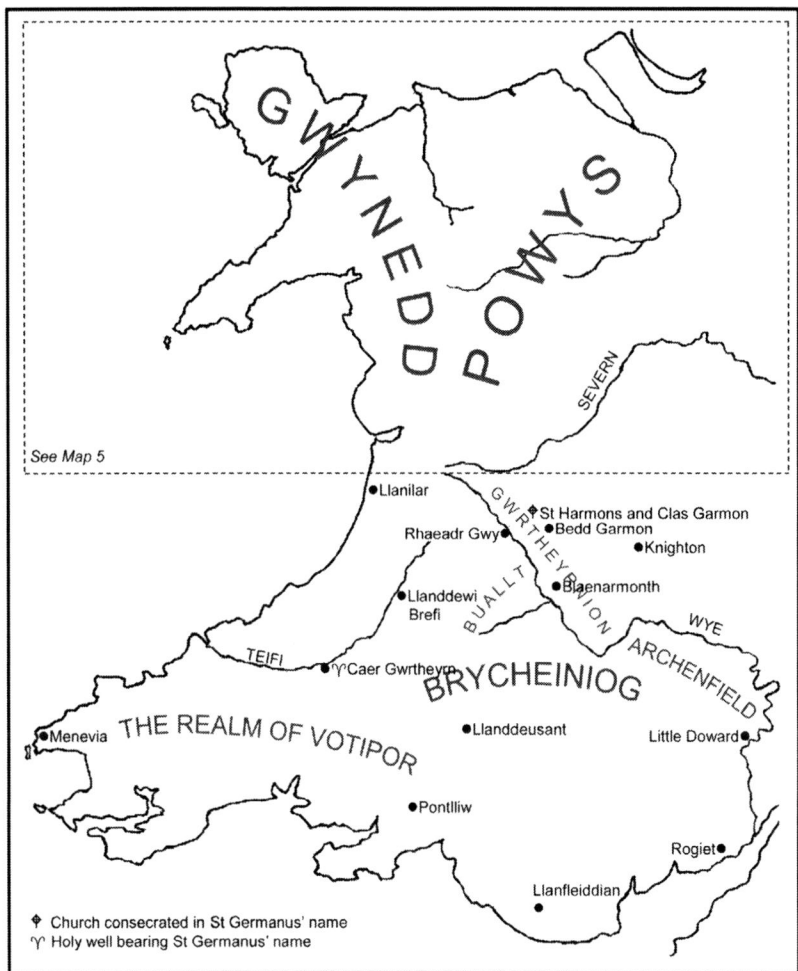

Map 4: Evidence of St Germanus in South Wales and the Marches

247

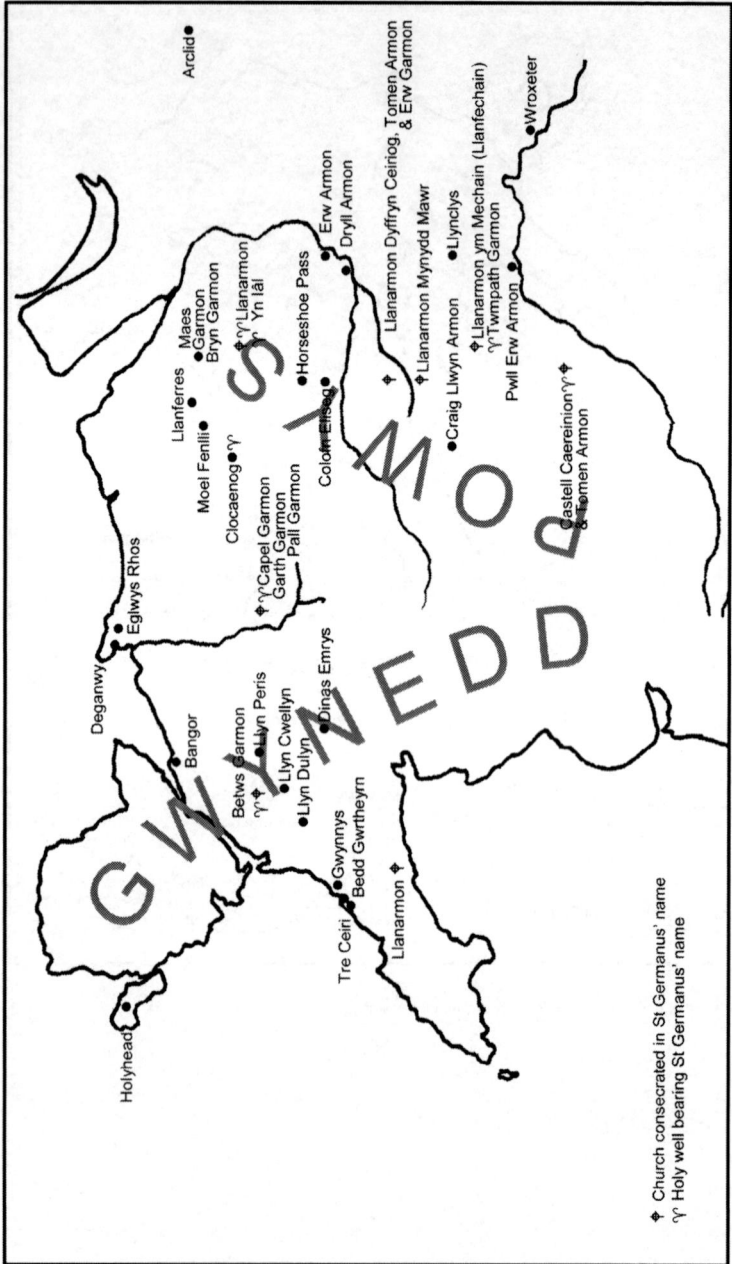

Map 5: Evidence of St Germanus in North Wales and the Marches

Labels on map:

Arclid

Wroxeter

Erw Armon
Dryll Armon

Llanarmon Dyffryn Ceiriog, Tomen Armon & Erw Garmon

Horseshoe Pass

ϒϒLlanarmon ϒn Iâl

Llanarmon Mynydd Mawr

Llanarmon ym Mechain (Llanfechain)
ϒϒLlynclys

Maes Garmon
Bryn Garmon

Llanferres

Craig Llwyn Armon

Moel Fenlli

ϒϒTwmpath Garmon
Pwll Erw Armon

Clocaenogϒϒ

Colomendy
Pall Garmon

ϒϒCapel Garmon
Garth Garmon

Castell Caereinionϒϒ
& Tomen Armon

Eglwys Rhos

Deganwy

Bangor

Llyn Peris

Betws Garmon
ϒϒ

Llyn Cwellyn
Llyn Dulyn

Dinas Emrys

Tre Ceiri

Gwynnys
Bedd Gwrtheyrn

Llanarmon

Holyhead

SYMODD

GWYNEDD

✠ Church consecrated in St Germanus' name
ϒ Holy well bearing St Germanus' name

248

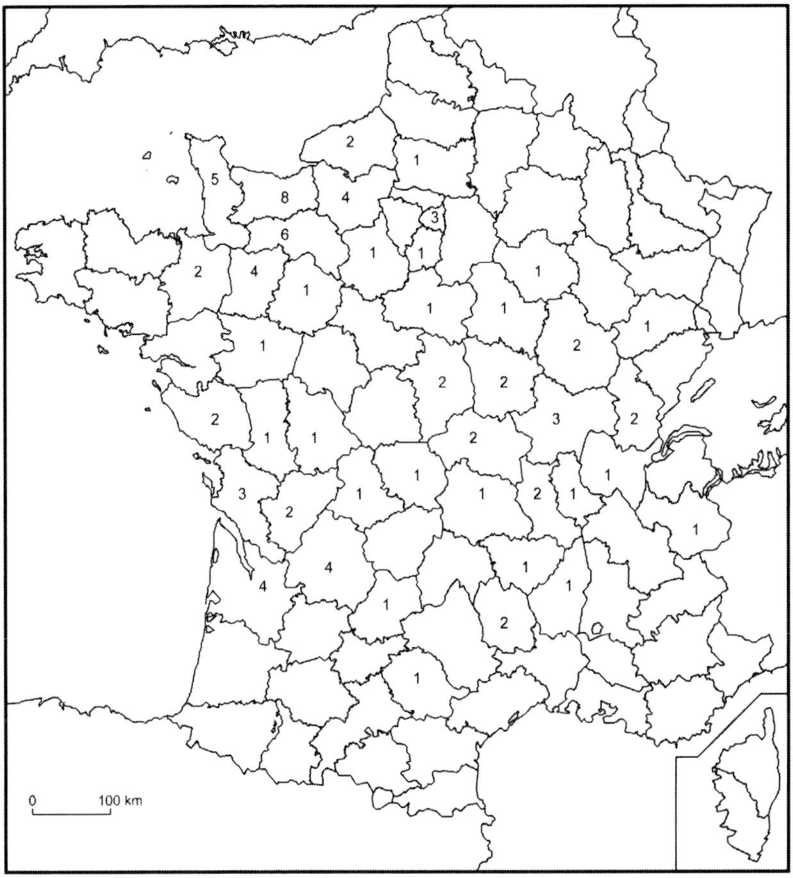

Map 6: Communities in France and Brittany whose names begin with Saint Germain (by *départment*).

Index.

Auxerre (Autessiodunum) 8-12, 19, 21-22, 28-29, 40, 52-53, 57, 63, 64, 131, 134-142 *passim*, 162, 173, 221-224 *passim*; Archdeacon of 135
Auxiliaris 21
Auxilius 140
Baia 73
Bale, John 31
Bangor (Arfon) 117, 195
Bangor Is-coed 110, 221
Barbarian Conspiracy 65
Bardsey, Abbey of 151; island of 177, 194
Baring-Gould, S. 59
Baptism 18, 42, 61, 75, 117, 155
Bauneville-sur-Mer 168
Bavaria 216
Bax Farm 36
Bedd Garmon 129, 157-158, 232
Bedd Gelert see St Celer, grave
Bedd Gwrtheyrn 76, 169
Bedd Illtud *see* St Illtud, grave
Bedd Twrog *see* St Twrog, grave
Bede 39, 44, 108
Belgium 29, 37
Beli ap Benlli Gawr 74
Bell 134, 150
Bendigeidfran 75
Benedict of Auxerre 166
Benedict of Gloucester 129
Benlli the Giant (Benlli Gawr) 66-68, 72-74 , 77, 81, 226; Moel Fenlli 73; Llys Fenlli 73
Berwyn 149
Bethlehem 215
Betws Garmon 142, 150-151, 189-190, 194-195, 232

Ephesus 111; Ecumenical Council of 96, 218
Epirichus, father of St Lupus 131
Epitoma Chronicon 54, 106
Epponiacus 64
Eraclius of Hippo, Bishop 120
Erging 170
Erw Armon 152, 156
Erw Garmon 154
Escolives-Sainte Camille 134
Essex 166
Eucherius of Lérins, Bishop of Lyons 43, 119
Euchologion 161
Eudoxia 50
Eulogius, Metropolitan of Caesarea 94
Euodius 30
Euric the Visigoth 79, 220
Eusebius 32
Eusebius of Vercelli 127
Exeter, cathedral 223; Diocese of 162
Exeter Relic List 162, 165
Exuperantius 51, 125, 217
Faganus *see* St Ffagan
Farinmail 71
Fastidius, Bishop 103
Fatalis 103
Faulkbourne 166
Faustus of Riez 71, 77-79, 82, 83, 119, 122, 216-221 *passim*
Ffair y Bol 154
Ffynnon Armon *see* St Germanus, wells
Ffynnon Armon, Aber 151
Ffynnon Llugwy 192
Fiacc 138, 139

237

Lérins 78, 98, 119, 131, 137, 138, 186
Lethia 138, 139
Levellers 113
Levison, Wilhelm 60
Lewis Glyn Cothi 173-178
Lewis, Saunders 180-181, 195
Lhuyd, Edward 83, 142, 143, 151, 152, 159, 187-188
Liber Praedestinatus 107
Liber Regularum 105
Licinius, Emperor 213, 214
Lincoln 70, 75
Lincolnshire 166
Lipari 118
Litorus 51, 219
Little Doward Hill 170
Life of Holy King Solomon of Brittany 51
Life of St Gurthiern 84
Llanarmon (Eifionydd) 150, 194
Llanarmon Dyffryn Ceiriog 154, 155, 232
Llanarmon Fach *see* Llanarmon Mynydd Mawr
Llanarmon Mynydd Mawr 149, 154-155
Llanarmon ym Mechain 155, 232
Llanarmon yn Iâl 41, 149, 152-154, 174, 184, 188-189, 232
Llanberis 156
Llanbister 157
Llandaff 130
Llanddeusant 77
Llanddewi Brefi 228, 232 *see also* Brefi
Llandegla 152, 153, 184
Llandrinio 156
Llanelyddan 133
Llanerfyl 149

Loch Carman see Loch Garman
Loch Garman 165, 238
London 36, 75
Lothair of Auxerre, Abbot 57
Lucius, King 182
Lugudunensis Senonia 29
Lullingstone 36
Lyons (Lugudunum) 21, 43, 54, 55, 63, 73
Mabinogi 75
Mac Colgan, Séan 224
Mâcon 131, 132
Maelgwn Gwynedd 83
Maelor Gymraeg 152
Maes Garmon 41, 143, 150, 152, 192, 223, 224, 232
Maes Mawr 73, 74
Maes-y-gwaelod 158
Magnus Maximus (Macsen Wledig) 45, 50, 82, 110, 215, 216
Main Meirion 73
Malew 164
Mamertinus 58
Man, Isle of 164-165, 224
Mani 90
Manicheanism 117
Manicheans 89, 94, 98
Marcus Aurelius, Emperor 213
Marcus the Welshman, Bishop 57, 64
Marianus 31, 53
Marius Mercator 89
Marmoutier 118
Marseilles 42, 118
Marske-by-the-Sea 167
Marteg, River 157

214; chapels of 163, 166, 184, 231; derivation of name 28-29; exorcisms 11-12, 15, 20, 24, 26; Feasts of 149, 153-157 *passim*, 162, 163, 164, 175, 180; grave of 154, 157, 162, 221, 222; Hallelujah Victory 18-19, 41, 42, 61, 65, 81, 149-154 *passim*, 181, 218, 223, 230; healings 11, 13, 16, 17, 20-28 *passim*, 172 in Britain 14-19, 21-22, 41, 52-63 *passim*, 101, 104, 107, 108, 122, 124, 130, 134, 135, 149, 180-187 *passim*, 218, 219, 231, 237; marriage 8; Massilians and 101, 122; miracles 16-17, 19-20, 25-26, 52-68 *passim*, 70, 166, 222; monasticism 127, 129; monastery of 10, 31, 52, 222, 223, 224; mounds and hills 152-156 passim, 160, 229-236; parents of 64, 188; poverty 9, 19, 24-25, 121; relics 27-28, 52-53, 142, 162, 165, 166, 222, 223; repose of 27, 51, 219; St David of Wales and 225-242 *passim*; secular career 8-9, 29-30, 31, 48, 56, 64, 125; *torgoch* and 142, 189-191; troparion to 7, 195-196; wells of 151-159 *passim*, 169

St Irenaeus of Lyons 32, 43, 213
St Isidore of Seville 56
St Jerome 29, 35, 90-93 *passim*, 106-110 *passim*, 118, 156, 215, 217
St John Cassian 29, 43, 59, 79, 98, 108, 118-122 *passim*, 186, 221
St John Chrysostom 93, 106, 216
St John of Colonia 30
St Kentigern, *Life* of 235
St-Loup 131-132
St Lupus of Troyes 14-16, 19, 33-37 *passim*, 44, 56, 63, 84, 101, 119-134 *passim*, 141, 164, 165, 180, 182-187 *passim*, 231; Annianus and 133; father of 131; *Life* of 131, 186; wife of 131
St Macarius, Homilies of 123
St Magnance 134
St Mark the Evangelist 141, 186
St Martin of Tours 30, 31, 37, 38, 41, 43, 51, 61, 63, 110, 118, 121, 127, 172-173, 215; Church at Areis 133; *Life* of 55, 108, 215
St Michael, chapel of 163
St Neot 164
St Neots (Cornwall) 163-164
St Ninnocha 143
St Non 177-178
St Pachomius 118
St Paisius Velichovsky 115
St Pallaye 134
St Patrick 48, 71, 133-143 *passim*, 164, 167, 237; *Confession* of 135; *Hymn* to 138; *Letter to Coroticus* 135, 138; *Life* of 137, 138, 139; *Sayings* of 138, 139
St Paul Aurelian 130; *Life* of 130
St Paula of Bethlehem 101

St Paulinus of Nola 50
St Paulinus of Wales 129, 130, 180, 227, 228
St Peris 142
St Peter, Church of 64
St Peter Chrysologus 50
St Petroc 161; chapel of 163
St Rhedyw 142-143, 188, 190-192
St Salvian of Marseilles 121
St Samson 127, 129; *Life* of 77, 129, 130, 158
St Seraphim of Sarov 115
St Severinus of Passau 132
St Severus of Trier 21, 44, 101, 132, 219, 220
St Silin 155
St Tathan of Gwent 72
St Teilo 129
St Twrog, grave of 158
St Victor, Abbey of 118
St Vincent of Lérins 100, 120
St Wethenye, chapel of 163
Sts Cosmas and Damian 31
Sts Gervasius and Protasius 49
Saint-Germain-des-Vaux 33
Saint's Crossing, The 153
Salisbury 166
Sandbach 126
Sant of Ceredigion 237
Saône 21
Sardica, Council of 101
Sarn Sws 149
Saxons 17-18, 44, 45, 56, 61, 65, 69, 75, 165, 180, 182, 214-221 *passim*
Scothorne 166
Scotists 121

Tremorze, Sir Nicholas *see* Tamworth, Sir Nicholas 162
Tre'r Ceiri 76
Tredegar, Lord 160
Treves 73, 110
Triadis Thaumaturga 224
Trier (Augusta Treverorum) 44, 45, 118, 214
Troyes (Trecassina) 29, 131-133 *passim*; Diocese of 131
Tudur Llwyd of Bodidris 179; Dafydd ap 180
Turin 39
Twmpath chwarae 232-233
Twmpath Garmon *see* St Germanus, mounds and hills
Tyrrhenian Sea 118, 137-140 *passim*, 217
Urbagen 81
Urban of Llandaff, Bishop 129; Geoffrey, brother of 129
Urmonoc 130
Ursus, Bishop of Mâcon 131
Usk Valley 143
Ussher, Archbishop James 41, 121-122, 124, 130, 141, 152, 185, 223
Uther (Pendragon) 170
Vaison, Synod of 44
Valence 122; Synod of 101, 221
Valens, Emperor 214
Valentinian III, Emperor 25, 28, 47, 50, 51, 103, 218, 219, 220
Valentinian, Patrician 139
Valentius 214
Vallis Rosina 141
Valor Ecclesiasticus 153
Vandals 47, 216, 218, 220
Vatican Council 121
Versailles 168, 169

Lightning Source UK Ltd.
Milton Keynes UK
UKOW050817301212

204217UK00006B/13/P

9 789081 155588